NO MORE TAXES

AN EXPOSE BY
JOHN PAUL MITCHELL

Written and published by John Paul Mitchell

Printed by Lulu Press

*A definitive look at the system of taxation and money
from a spiritual and historical perspective.*

Copyright © 2008 John Paul Mitchell

ISBN: 978–0–6151–9880–4

Printed in the United States of America

Contents

Compliance Without Resistance   1

World's Most Famous Tax Protester   5

Give Unto Caesar   9

The Temple Moneychangers   13

Capernaum Synagogue Tax   21

A Distaste For Tax Collectors   25

Sovereign Individuality   31

A Brief History of Taxes   41

A New World   47

Evils of a Centralized Bank   51

The U.S. Constitution and Taxes   **63**

Black Hand: American Style   **69**

How Citizens Are Negatively Affected   **75**

A Tax Free World   **85**

Appendix   **91**

    No More Taxes 91

    Interview with a Tax Protester 95

    Rothschild's 25-Point Plan 108

Introduction

The fruits of what eventually became this book started out simply as an article[1], with the same title, that exposed taxation as extortion. This uniquely spiritual and historical perspective told of each human being's innately and benevolent rights of peace, happiness, property, and liberty. The original article was written shortly after I left my spiritual mentor in the latter half of 2007. It was my attempt to summarize my realizations that compliance with tax collection was like letting yourself be robbed at gunpoint.

My conviction became even more founded when a fellow tax protester, Ned Netterville, made personal contact with me. God afforded me the ability to grow in my realization that tax is theft with this new friendship. Through Ned's unending support I was able to remain motivated throughout the entire writing process. From start to finish, the initial manuscript took approximately three weeks. Besides Ned, I owe my unconditional gratitude to God, the One Great Power, for continually providing divine inspiration and just the right word when it was needed.

---

[1] See the Appendix for *No More Taxes*, the article that inspired this book.

As the reader adventures from chapter to chapter, a progressive pattern is realized. The book flows in a simple and realistic way. The first half of the book, consisting of seven chapters, highlights the spiritual perspective of this expose. The latter half, which consists of chapters eight through fourteen, is the historical vantage of governments throughout history and their methods of taxation. The seventh chapter, *Sovereign Individuality*, is one of the most important parts. It gives the reader the tools to live a life of non–state self–governance through independence, respect, responsibility, honesty, and a keen awareness about our tax–driven world.

Most readers when finished will be utterly appalled by government, bankers, and taxes. More than likely, you will never want to pay taxes again!

Part One

Compliance Without Resistance

Along the journey of life, from infancy to adulthood, we encounter a constant bombardment of conditionings in our civilized societies. Whether these societal, cultural, or political conditionings are good or evil, true or deceptive, pure or impure, they vie for our awareness and have the ability to manipulate our being. From morning to night, there is someone or some group wanting us to do what they want us to do for their benefit, pleasure, or both. There is no escaping it, not even for a moment.

The less we ask and the more we willingly or unconsciously comply makes it that much easier for the control–seekers to dictate our thoughts, our actions, our choices, our lives. It does not matter if these thoughts, actions, or choices will benefit us or not, it only matters that our compliance comes without resistance.

Government is the dark spawn of human civilization because it demands compliance without resistance.

Once a government is solidly established with legislation and measures of violent enforcement in place, it can easily dictate how free their citizens are. Government becomes very dangerous when the people are no longer in charge and a select few reign with to-talitarian authority. Fascist governments and dictatorships literally enslave people through fear, force, manipulation of the law, and extortion in the guise of taxation.

Taxation is the system to measure compliance with fascist rule. It is the means to fund selfish governmental activities that do not protect the people nor sustain the law. Throughout history all kinds of governmental systems have used the funds of their extortion rackets abusively.

The United States of America is no different. The U.S. Congress prepares, writes, and enacts tax codes that have absolutely no found-ation in the United States Constitution. The Internal Revenue Ser-vice (IRS) as the *La Mano Nera* or "the Black Hand"[1] of the United States federal government, enforces tax rules to extort and swindle hard–earned money from the American people. Every sin-gle penny collected is deposited into the Federal Reserve, a non–governmental agency and banking system.

Not a single dollar of taxpayer money is used for the branches,

---

[1]The roots of the Black Hand can be traced to Sicily where it began in the 1750's. It is a type of extortion where a letter is delivered to the victim. The envelope would have either a smoking gun, hangman's noose, or black fist sym-bol. The letter would demand a specific amount of money to be delivered to a pre-determined location. If the victim did not comply with the demands the letter detailed threats of bodily harm or death.

agencies, or services of the federal government. Nor is a single penny is dumped into the military operations that incite animosity and create enemies by operating on foreign soil.

The leaders of the United States continually borrow money from the Federal Reserve. This central banking system is not owned and operated by the federal government. It is controlled by a group of powerful bankers and banking interests in partnership with the U.S. President and Senate. Whenever the federal government needs more money, they rely solely on the Federal Reserve bank to lend the desired funds. This money is created out of thin air, having no more value than Monopoly game money; the currency is not backed by gold or silver.

But it is best you forget about these truths. The government would rather you put this book down, forget about the contents of its pages. What you have read could get you in severe trouble with authoritarian control, maybe arrested and brought to trial for treason as a "traitor of the state" or an "enemy combatant." In the United States, treason is still punishable by death[2].

---

[2]U.S. Code states, "Whoever, owing allegiance to the United States, levies war against them or adheres to their enemies, giving them aid and comfort within the United States or elsewhere, is guilty of treason and shall suffer death, or shall be imprisoned not less than five years and fined under this title but not less than $10,000; and shall be incapable of holding any office under the United States."

World's Most Famous Tax Protester

For a moment, imagine this dramatic scene:

A bloody, beaten, and weakened man is hurried through a raging mob of men and women. The man is paraded in front of the provincial governor of an occupied Middle East nation. There is shouting, screaming, and vulgar remarks hurled from the verbally abusive crowd.

A select few men dressed eloquently in religious garb stand at the front near a stone staircase. The religious men openly declare, almost in unison, that the man is guilty of claiming to be the Messiah, or Israel's rightful King. They also tell the governor that this Messiah has thwarted the power of Rome and told the Jews to avoid paying the Roman poll tax.

As the accused man stands there dripping sweat and losing blood, the governor begins to interrogate him. He asks if he is the King of the Jews. Without reluctance, the man flippantly remarks, "You say so." Questions are asked regarding the man's teaching of rebellion, yet the Messiah remains silent so as not to incriminate himself.

When the governor learns the tax resister is from Galilee, he sends the man to face trial before Herod Antipas, the tetrarch or ruler of Galilee. The religious men drag the tax resister in front of the tetrarch, who mocks and insults him. This continues until the ruler grows tired and turns him back over to the governor.

Again, the man is brought to the governor's palace. Pontius Pilate calls for the religious leaders, rulers of the quarters, and Jewish people to assemble for his verdict.

Pilate is about to release Jesus, but the religious leaders and Jewish people testify that he has incited rebellion with his teachings to not pay taxes. Because of this testimony from the people who witnessed Jesus teaching publicly, Pilate condemns him to death by crucifixion.

Tragically, Jesus was executed by the most horrific form of Roman capital punishment. This method of torture and execution was only reserved for slaves, rebels, and the worst criminals of non–Roman descent.

The premise of this story was inspired by Luke 23 from the New Testament in the Holy Bible.

Jesus as an illegal tax protester is a severe accusation and charge. A difficult lesson for the traditional Christian–oriented mind to fathom. Those who are familiar with modern Christian teachings might be appalled to discover Jesus taught his students, followers, and the Jewish people to avoid payment of taxes.

The arguments for this controversial portrayal of Jesus the Christ will be thoroughly reviewed in the next few chapters.

Give Unto Caesar

ARGUMENT #1: DENARIUS COINS

"Give to Caesar what is Caesar's, and to God what is God's" is one of the most famous sayings attributed to Jesus, a thought–provoking Rabbi revolutionist.

Though Matthew 22:21 is often quoted to credit the agenda of pastors, spiritual teachers, or government officials, the quote is usually taken out of context. When reading scripture, we should avoid isolation. Scripture isolation occurs when we take a verse out of context, not relying on the story or other stanzas that accompany the selected verse. By selectively choosing a piece of scripture and adding commentary, a person can make that scripture applicable to a variety of situations.

To fully appreciate Jesus' mastery of spoken language and his ability to disengage confrontation it is important to visit the following scene:

*Then the Pharisees went out and laid plans to trap him
in his words.*

*They sent their disciples to him along with the Hero-
dians.*

*"Teacher," they said, "we know you are a man of in-
tegrity and that you teach the way of God in accor-
dance with the truth. You aren't swayed by men, because you pay no attention to who they are.*

*Tell us then, what is your opinion? Is it right to pay
taxes to Caesar or not?"*

*But Jesus, knowing their evil intent, said, "You hyp-
ocrites, why are you trying to trap me? Show me the
coin used for paying the tax."*

*They brought him a denarius, and he asked them, "Whose
portrait is this? And whose inscription?"*

"Caesar's," they replied.

*Then he said to them, "Give to Caesar what is Cae-
sar's, and to God what is God's."*

*When they heard this, they were amazed. So they left
him and went away.*

Since Jesus' ministry must be examined primarily from a historical point of view, we should understand a few things about the
Roman occupation of ancient Israel and Judah.

In 63 BCE, Pompey conquered Jerusalem. At this time, Israel and Judah became the province of Judea. Non–citizens of Rome were obligated to pay a flat poll tax. Roman born men and women were exempt.

The Pharisees were a Jewish religious sect that severely opposed Jesus' teachings. When they sent their disciples cloaked in deception to Jesus, they deliberately praised the Rabbi to win his favor. However, this back–fired. Jesus was alert to the devious plan they set out to accomplish and realized their true intention.

The Pharisees, like other Jews, were aware Jesus taught people to not pay taxes to Rome or the Jewish Temple. Jesus foresaw the trap and exclaimed, "You hypocrites, why are you trying to trap me?"

If Jesus did not teach tax evasion and disobedience to Rome, why did he mention the Pharisees' and Herodians' evil intention to trap him?

If he taught compliance to taxation, then he would not feel the urgency to avoid entrapment of such a question. He would have simply answered, "Pay your taxes."

Rather, Jesus insisted his confronters bring a denarius coin to him. The denarius was the commonplace currency of the Roman Empire and the only acceptable coin for Roman poll tax payments. Greek and Jewish currency was unacceptable and had to be converted into denarius coins by the moneychangers, who operated their financial empire from the Jewish Temple in Jerusalem.

Once the coin was produced, Jesus asked the picture and inscription on it. The men sent to trap him, replied, "Caesar."

That is when Jesus masterfully responded, "Give to Caesar
what is Caesar's."

As the ruler of the Roman Empire, the currency used for exchange, legally belonged to Caesar. It may have belonged to Caesar in the same way as a corporation is "legally" a person—what
is called a legal fiction. The denarius coins Jesus mentions were
property of the Roman Empire.

If we take this teaching literally, there are only two logical ways
to ensure the Jewish people gave Caesar what belonged to him.

The first is to take all the denarius money from their moneybags
and deliver them to the tax collectors or dump their denarius on
Caesar's palace steps. This would require them to give all their
Roman currency back to Caesar.

The second is to convert all denarius money into Greek or Jewish currency. By liquidating denarius into another form of exchange, Jesus' followers could literally put denarius they possessed
back into circulation. This method would require them to convert
all their denarius, thus giving "to Caesar what is Caesars's," but
indirectly.

Nowhere in Jesus' statement does he say, "Give to Caesar what
Caesar requires of you." Therefore, the Rabbi revolutionist did
not directly answer the question presented to him, but avoided it
entirely while teaching about rebellion.

The Temple Moneychangers

ARGUMENT #2: JESUS ATTACKS THE MONEYCHANGERS

Again, imagine this heated scene:

After spending a few days with family, friends, and disciples in Capernaum, Jesus set out for Jerusalem. Upon arriving, he took a select group of disciples, including Peter–his personal bodyguard– to the Jewish Temple.

Immediately upon entering the sanctuary, the Rabbi revolution- ist took a bundle of cords. He created a whip and fiercely struck the floor near the moneychangers. He continued whipping the thick cords until priests, merchants, and Jews began to run and scatter.

In a fit of violent fury, Jesus overturned the tables of the money- changers. Coins went flying into the air and onto the ground. Ro- man, Greek, Jewish, and Tyrian money was scattered everywhere.

The moneychangers quickly stood, fearing Jesus would strike them. Fearfully looking into his eyes the men could see his anger. As they looked beyond him, they noticed a small band of men holding daggers and swords. Jesus' disciples were prepared and anxiously waiting.

Again, Jesus made another violent outburst. This time he knocked over the cages that held doves. He also let loose cattle and other animals being traded or sold.

Shouting so everybody present could hear, he exclaimed, "The Torah states, 'My house will be a house of prayer,'[1] but you have made it a den of thieves[2]."

This scene is related in all four Gospel accounts of the New Testament. Jesus, usually portrayed as peaceful and wise, dramatically belies that imagery by attacking the moneychangers on their home turf.

The Great Sanhedrin, an assembly of a High Priest, Vice Chief Justice, and sixty–nine general members, made a profit by renting space in the Temple to the moneychangers, who were the Jewish bankers and lenders of Judea. They operated primarily out of the Jewish Temple in Jerusalem. Within the Temple were large vaults that stored all types of currency, valuables, treasures, and artifacts.

In the days of Jesus, the Temple was known as a national treasury. There was a requirement that every adult male pay the Jewish

---

[1]Isaiah 56:7: "Even them will I bring to my holy mountain, and make them joyful in my house of prayer: their burnt offerings and their sacrifices shall be accepted upon mine altar; for mine house shall be called an house of prayer for all people."

[2]Jeremiah 7:11: "Is this house, which is called by my name, become a den of robbers in your eyes? Behold, even I have seen it, saith the LORD."

Temple Tax of a half shekel. Ordinary Jews had to pay this special tax if they wanted to pray, worship, and sacrifice during Passover.

Foreign currency was forbidden for the transaction and only a Jewish half shekel was acceptable. If a Jew had Greek or Roman coins, they had to convert that money into a half shekel. The bankers would charge a high fee to transfer from one currency to another, and rates were even higher during the busy Passover festival.

Exodus 30:12–14 states:

And the LORD spake unto Moses, saying,

When thou takest the sum of the children of Israel after their number, then shall they give every man a ransom for his soul unto the LORD, when thou numberest them; that there be no plague among them, when thou numberest them.

This they shall give, every one that passeth among them that are numbered, half a shekel after the shekel of the sanctuary: (a shekel is twenty gerahs:) an half shekel shall be the offering of the LORD.

Every one that passeth among them that are numbered, from twenty years old and above, shall give an offering unto the LORD.

The rich shall not give more, and the poor shall not give less than half a shekel, when they give an offering unto the LORD, to make an atonement for your souls.

> *And thou shalt take the atonement money of the children of Israel, and shalt appoint it for the service of the tabernacle of the congregation; that it may be a memorial unto the children of Israel before the LORD, to make an atonement for your souls.*

Prophet Ezra, the story compiler and redactor of the Torah, conveniently inserted the above passage into the Torah to justify the politics of collecting a mandatory tax. Only the priests and staff of the Jewish temple were exempt from paying it. The following passage from Ezra 7 is a letter composed by King Artaxerxes I[3] with his orders and stipulations regarding taxes:

> *Artaxerxes, king of kings, unto Ezra the priest, a scribe of the law of the God of heaven, perfect peace, and at such a time.*
>
> *I make a decree, that all they of the people of Israel, and of his priests and Levites, in my realm, which are minded of their own freewill to go up to Jerusalem, go with thee.*
>
> *Forasmuch as thou art sent of the king, and of his seven counsellors, to enquire concerning Judah and Jerusalem, according to the law of thy God which is in thine hand;*

[3] Artaxerxes I of Persia was the king of the Persian Empire from 465 BCE to 424 BCE. His father was Xerxes I of Persia.

And to carry the silver and gold, which the king and his counsellors have freely offered unto the God of Israel, whose habitation is in Jerusalem,

And all the silver and gold that thou canst find in all the province of Babylon, with the freewill offering of the people, and of the priests, offering willingly for the house of their God which is in Jerusalem:

That thou mayest buy speedily with this money bullocks, rams, lambs, with their meat offerings and their drink offerings, and offer them upon the altar of the house of your God which is in Jerusalem.

And whatsoever shall seem good to thee, and to thy brethren, to do with the rest of the silver and the gold, that do after the will of your God.

The vessels also that are given thee for the service of the house of thy God, those deliver thou before the God of Jerusalem.

And whatsoever more shall be needful for the house of thy God, which thou shalt have occasion to bestow, bestow it out of the king's treasure house.

And I, even I Artaxerxes the king, do make a decree to all the treasurers which are beyond the river, that whatsoever Ezra the priest, the scribe of the law of the God of heaven, shall require of you, it be done speedily,

Unto an hundred talents of silver, and to an hundred measures of wheat, and to an hundred baths of wine, and to an hundred baths of oil, and salt without prescribing how much.

Whatsoever is commanded by the God of heaven, let it be diligently done for the house of the God of heaven: for why should there be wrath against the realm of the king and his sons?

Also we certify you, that touching any of the priests and Levites, singers, porters, Nethinims, or ministers of this house of God, it shall not be lawful to impose toll, tribute, or custom, upon them.

And thou, Ezra, after the wisdom of thy God, that is in thine hand, set magistrates and judges, which may judge all the people that are beyond the river, all such as know the laws of thy God; and teach ye them that know them not.

And whosoever will not do the law of thy God, and the law of the king, let judgment be executed speedily upon him, whether it be unto death, or to banishment, or to confiscation of goods, or to imprisonment.

Blessed be the LORD God of our fathers, which hath put such a thing as this in the king's heart, to beautify the house of the LORD which is in Jerusalem:

And hath extended mercy unto me before the king,

and his counsellors, and before all the king's mighty princes. And I was strengthened as the hand of the LORD my God was upon me, and I gathered together out of Israel chief men to go up with me.

Ezra had the blessings of the Persian King and the high–esteem of over 5,000 Israelite exiles. Artaxerxes sent Ezra on a political pilgrimage to Jerusalem so he would win favor with the Jews in the Holy City. Ezra performed exceedingly well and was even able to establish a method of collecting additional money for his mission.

So when Jesus attacked the moneychangers in the Temple he was violently protesting the unethical business practices of the bankers, how they stole from the Jewish people (see Exodus 20:15,17[4]; Deuteronomy 5:19,21[5]), and the taxation Ezra established through a foreign power's political agenda.

---

[4]Exodus 20:15,17: "Thou shalt not steal. Thou shalt not covet thy neighbour's house, thou shalt not covet thy neighbour's wife, nor his manservant, nor his maidservant, nor his ox, nor his ass, nor any thing that is thy neighbour's."

[5]Deuteronomy 5:19,21: "Neither shalt thou steal. Neither shalt thou desire thy neighbour's wife, neither shalt thou covet thy neighbour's house, his field, or his manservant, or his maidservant, his ox, or his ass, or any thing that is thy neighbour's."

Capernaum Synagogue Tax

ARGUMENT #3: TO PAY OR NOT TO PAY?

Capernaum was a settlement on the Sea of Galilee, a city of the Judea province. When Jesus began his public ministry, he selected Capernaum as his headquarters. Many of Jesus' first disciples lived in this fishing town.

Early in the first century a synagogue was constructed by a Roman centurion and his soldiers (see Luke 7:1–5)[1]. Jesus regularly read from the Torah and taught about the Lord at this same synagogue. As a Rabbi, he had a close professional relationship with the other Rabbis and priests at that location of worship.

---

[1]Luke 7:1–5: "Now when he had ended all his sayings in the audience of the people, he entered into Capernaum. And a certain centurion's servant, who was dear unto him, was sick, and ready to die. And when he heard of Jesus, he sent unto him the elders of the Jews, beseeching him that he would come and heal his servant. And when they came to Jesus, they besought him instantly, saying, That he was worthy for whom he should do this: For he loveth our nation, and he hath built us a synagogue."

An important event happened near this synagogue. Matthew 17:24–27 reads:

> *After Jesus and his disciples arrived in Capernaum, the collectors of the two–drachma tax came to Peter and asked, "Doesn't your teacher pay the temple tax?"*
>
> *"Yes, he does," he replied.*
>
> *When Peter came into the house, Jesus was the first to speak. "What do you think, Simon?" he asked. "From whom do the kings of the earth collect duty and taxes from their own sons or from others?"*
>
> *"From others," Peter answered.*
>
> *"Then the sons are exempt," Jesus said to him.*
>
> *"But so that we may not offend them, go to the lake and throw out your line. Take the first fish you catch; open its mouth and you will find a four–drachma coin. Take it and give it to them for my tax and yours."*

The Greek drachma was the commonplace currency of Greece and often circulated in Galilee and other parts of Judea. In Jerusalem, the Temple Tax could only be paid with a Jewish half shekel, however, in Capernaum, the synagogue was more lenient and accepted two drachma coins for their tax. Then the synagogue was responsible for paying their dues to the Jerusalem Temple, keeping a smaller portion for themselves to perform regular maintenance on the building.

Jesus waited in Peter's house. While Peter was returning home, walking near the Capernaum synagogue, he was approached by Publicans. They confronted him on the matter of the synagogue tax. He quickly responded that his master teacher pays the tax, answering a question on his own authority.

Upon returning home, Jesus questioned Peter immediately about the tax issue. He asked Peter, "From whom do the kings of the earth collect duty and taxes, from their own sons or from others?"

Peter answered, "From others." And Jesus replied, "Then the sons are exempt," meaning the Jews were exempt from the current system of taxation imposed by the Great Sanhedrin and money-changers of the Jerusalem Temple.

However, since Jesus knew Peter already told the Publicans that Jesus would pay the temple tax, he instructed Peter to pay that one time by retrieving money from a fish's mouth. Because of Peter's answer, Jesus was now obligated to pay. Otherwise, if Jesus failed to pay the tax, he could later face harassment from the Publicans or lose his special privilege to speak in the Capernaum synagogue.

It is interesting to note that neither Jesus nor Peter worked for the four–drachma coin. Jesus told Peter where to easily find this fish and what to do with it. It is like the Greek coin magically appeared as Jesus promised with little effort or hunting on Peter's part.

Why would Jesus, if he were a tax protester, instruct his disciple to pay the tax for them both?

Through investigating American tax protesters, it is interesting to see that some advocate tax evasion or resistance, however, in practicality, they pay their federal taxes. Why would anyone advocating tax resistance do this?

These individuals, by speaking out against the system, bring attention to themselves from the government. Since the government has authoritarian control and power to punish, these tax protesters play it safe by giving the minimum tax. As a tax protester, it is a wise political move to do this, so the protester can continue speaking freely and publicly against the government.

We can assume Jesus had a very similar motive, that it was political and by paying the temple tax that one time, it was worth it to continue the ministry.

A Distaste For Tax Collectors

ARGUMENT #4: Tax Collector as Protypical Sinner

Frederic Bastiat, a French economist and philosopher, wrote and published a pamphlet in 1850 entitled *The Law*. In this small but informative booklet, he coined the term "legal plunder" to describe the system of mandatory taxation.

There can be a law formulated by a government to justify taxation, but it does not make it ethical or right in the eyes of God. Fault also falls upon the tax collector who steals from his fellow citizen, enforcing illicit legal plunder. By merely working as a tax collector for a profession, a person is committing a severe and grave sin against humanity.

By examining a few select sayings of Jesus, we can clearly see how the Rabbi revolutionist held tax collectors in a position of contempt, and often referred to them as sinners.

"If you love those who love you, what reward will you get? Are not even the tax collectors doing that?" (Matthew 5:46)

"When the Pharisees saw this, they asked his disciples, Why does your teacher eat with tax collectors and sinners?

On hearing this, Jesus said, It is not the healthy who need a doctor, but the sick.

But go and learn what this means: I desire mercy, not sacrifice. For I have not come to call the righteous, but sinners." (ibid. 9:11–13)

The Pharisees on many occasions spied or received communication that Jesus was socializing and dining with tax collectors, prostitutes, and sinners. Though Jesus spoke of them negatively in his public discourses, he was quite friendly to them and enjoyed their company. It may seem hypocritical that Jesus dined and drank with tax collectors, however, to his credit, he socialized so they would come under the influence of his divine teachings.

And the power of his teachings held weight in the minds of at least two tax collectors. Early in Jesus' mission, he was able to convert Levi, a Jewish Publican later known as Matthew, into his group. Jesus later selected Matthew as one of the twelve Apostles or witnesses of his inner circle. The Apostles often congregated in Matthew's dwelling to eat, drink, and listen to Jesus teach.

Zacchaeus' conversion story is equally impressive, if not more so. He was the Head Publican in Jericho. When it came to taxes in this export city, he was the boss. He had the final say and could increase taxes at will. The people hated Zacchaeus immensely and there was always someone slandering him.

Luke 9:1–10 states:

And Jesus entered and passed through Jericho.

And, behold, there was a man named Zacchaeus, which was the chief among the publicans, and he was rich.

And he sought to see Jesus who he was; and could not for the press, because he was little of stature.

And he ran before, and climbed up into a sycomore tree to see him: for he was to pass that way.

And when Jesus came to the place, he looked up, and saw him, and said unto him, Zacchaeus, make haste, and come down; for to day I must abide at thy house.

And he made haste, and came down, and received him joyfully.

And when they saw it, they all murmured, saying, That he was gone to be guest with a man that is a sinner.

And Zacchaeus stood, and said unto the Lord: Behold, Lord, the half of my goods I give to the poor; and if I have taken any thing from any man by false accusation, I restore him fourfold.

And Jesus said unto him, This day is salvation come to this house, forsomuch as he also is a son of Abraham.

For the Son of man is come to seek and to save that which was lost.

Even Jericho's head tax collector realized his fault, admitting he stole from his fellow brethren. It is amazing that a man of Zaachaeus' position would convert within an instant and confess he was wrong for supporting the system of taxation.

Zacchaeus' new friendship certainly received a lot of public attention through the province of Judea with word spreading quickly to the Great Sanhedrin of the Jewish Court. For the Jewish Court, it was a severe blow to their ability to suppress Jesus' ever–increasing following. Daily, his followers were gathering in larger numbers to show support and learn directly from the most talked about Rabbi in all of Judea.

How could you ignore Jesus? He taught a message that promised an ever–lasting kingdom that raised up the individual to sovereignty through God, the One Great Power.

Man can suppress and create unethical, life–stealing laws all they want. They can tax every single citizen, beat them up and jail them for not complying, and instill fear into the general public. But they can never steal away the spark of life that truly belongs to God.

The psalmist of Psalms 24:1 eloquently wrote:

> *"The earth is the LORD's, and everything in it, the world, and all who live in it."*

When you steal from man, no matter the reason or method, you are stealing from God.

Sovereign Individuality

What is sovereign individuality?

To help our understanding, let us study the following definitions:

sov·er·eign [sov–er–in]

1. a person who has sovereign power or authority.

2. having supreme rank, power, or authority.

3. self–governing; independent.

in·di·vid·u·al·i·ty [in–duh–vij–oo–al–i–tee]

1. a person or thing of individual or distinctive character.

2. state or quality of being individual; existence as a distinct individual.

3. the interests of the individual as distinguished from the interests of the community.

31

Furthermore, sovereign individuality is an inherent right belonging to every single man, woman, and child. Taxing a person cannot take away their personal sovereignty. Nor can unjustly arresting a person make them any less a king or queen of their own self. Even if these acts demean a person, they will never rip the spark of life from their soul.

This explicit right is granted to every living soul by Eloi Abba[1] – God the Father. And it is only further strengthened when the individual recognizes the connectedness of self with community, and self with the Supreme Architect.

Jesus, a true messenger of God, spoke of this when being interrogated by Pontius Pilate. John 18:33–36 states:

> *Pilate then went back inside the palace, summoned Jesus and asked him, Are you the king of the Jews?*
>
> *Is that your own idea, Jesus asked, or did others talk to you about me?*
>
> *Am I a Jew? Pilate replied. It was your people and your chief priests who handed you over to me. What is it you have done?*
>
> *Jesus said, My kingdom is not of this world. If it were, my servants would fight to prevent my arrest by the Jews. But now my kingdom is from another place.*

---

[1] Author's Note: *Eloi Abba* is the unique name I personally use for God. In Hebrew and Aramaic, it means "God, the Father".

What is this other place? It would be heaven.

The mystery of heaven has confounded the minds of philosophers, religious adherents, and scholars for centuries. Heaven is not only a place within the metaphysical universe, it is also a state of being reached through progressive development, refinement, and devotion to God the Father.

As the founder and teacher of Illumina[2], a powerful self–transformation and personal development regimen, I originally chose four cornerstone philosophies when developing the system. They are as follows: self–ownership, self–reflection, self–mastery, and self–illumination. In this book and chapter, I will only discuss self–ownership in detail because it applies to sovereign individuality. This topic is gravely important while thoroughly examining legally sanctioned theft.

In self–ownership, the primary focus is on the individual and its functioning within society and in the world.

This tenet of Illumina wisdom can be further divided into five principle categories:

1. Independence

2. Responsibility

3. Respectfulness

4. Liberty

5. Awareness

---

[2] *Illumina* in Latin means "glow" or "light."

The first virtue of self–ownership is independence. This is the ability and practicality of being self–dependent, taking the necessary steps to learn, grow, maintain wellness, and provide for oneself. It is alright to be co–dependent on our parents and teachers, but when we reach a certain age, we must live and make decisions for ourselves. We cannot rely on our governments to provide for us, we must do that on our own. It is our responsibility to do what no one else will do for us.

On this note, responsibility is the second virtue. It requires taking ownership for what you think, say, and do, even if the consequences are restrictive, harmful, and unpleasant to oneself. A responsible person will face the the repercussions of their mistakes, whether mild or severe. It is through our mistakes and their consequences that we learn to really incorporate a responsible attitude, and act accordingly.

Those who are firmly grounded in the wisdom of self–ownership have a natural respect for other people. This is the third virtue, a great one that produces many benefits for self and society. A sovereign individual prides himself on not intentionally robbing a person of life, nor harming their body, well–being, liberty, and property. The ethic of reciprocity is a fundamental moral principle and practice displaying respectfulness in the most humanitarian way. Arguably, it is the most essential quality and basis for the concept of human rights. It should be the Golden Rule that guides our every word and deed.

In Luke 6:31, Jesus states this Golden Rule simply:

"Do to others as you would have them do to you."

If we are respectful of others and do not impose intentional wrongdoing or harm upon that person, then we allow that person to retain their full liberties. However, if we harm that person or steal from them, then we are robbing them of their right to personal liberty. As a person that enjoys the freedom to do as he or she wishes, a sovereign individual never wants to intrude on the divine right of freedom.

Liberty, the fourth virtue, comes through practice of ethical behavior. This is something that thieves, murderers, rapists, tax collectors, tyrants, and dictators cannot grasp. They would prefer to rob life rather than uphold life.

Through ever–increasing awareness of self, community, and society, we can make better decisions for ourselves and others. For example, if we were to see a loved one negatively affected by our hurtful words, we can learn from this mistake and create a loving environment of acceptance, tolerance, and thoughtful communication. The Buddhist discipline of mindfulness can be taken from the meditation cushion to thoughtfulness in word and action. The sovereign individual comes full circle; awareness manifests as respectfulness.

Frank Chodorov, author and anti–tax activist had this to say regarding life, the individual, and property:

"If we assume that the individual has an indisputable right to life, we must concede that he has a similar right to the enjoyment of the products of his labor. This we call a property right. The absolute right to property follows from the original right to life because one without the other is meaningless; the means to life must be identified with life itself." – Taxation is Robbery, 1947

In the next chapter, we shall learn how ancient and modern civilizations violated and disregarded the sovereign individual in the wake of thievery and extortion. However, as you read the last half of the book, please keep in mind how you factor into the equation. Do you tolerate the government's authorization and involvement in legalized theft? Though you do not directly steal and take money from your neighbor or your community, how are you responsible for supporting a system of extortion?

When we live in a welfare state when individuals of our society are dependent on the government handing out freebies for the sake of livelihood, it determines our collective ignorance and irresponsibility toward the apparent theft running rampant in our society. It shows little responsibility on our part to pay into the system, let alone our level of respect for ourselves and humanity. Every time we allow the government to steal from us and use their government budget on welfare programs, we are harming our society further. We take from the majority and give to a minority. All we do is shift the money around from one pocket to another; we are no better than a robber who breaks into and loots a house in the cover and silence of night.

The knowledge between right and wrong is a widening gap that hides the truth. This especially happens when the people of a nation willingly allow themselves to be taxed. If we give money to our government for taxes or support government approved welfare programs, then we are co–responsible with our leaders and elected officials for committing a severe abomination against mankind. Stealing is abhorred by the tenets of all the world's major religions and numerous spiritual paths.

As a person strives to achieve and maintain sovereign individuality, it is important to examine one's life and whether it is aligned with the core values of independence, responsibility, respectfulness, liberty, and awareness. If we stop and ask ourselves right now, "Is my life dignified and honorable?" will our being echo a yes or no? If yes, then we are fine in the sight of God, knowing without a shadow of a doubt we are not indirectly sanctioning theft and other unethical actions. If no, then what we can do to reform ourselves, reclaim our individual sovereignty, and shed off the bondage of man–created systems?

God willing, by the end of this book, you will have the answer to the latter question.

Part Two

A Brief History of Taxes

Taxes are a problem for most working class people and anyone who makes a substantial amount from wages and investments. Not surprisingly, taxation problems date back to the earliest point of our recorded histories.

Let us examine a list of ancient and modern civilizations and how they forcefully imposed taxes on their subjects, slaves, and citizens:

Ancient Egypt

The first recorded references of a system of taxation dates to 3000–2800 BCE, the first dynasty of the Old Kingdom in Ancient Egypt. Administrative and literary texts, letters, and scenes from tombs all provide definite archaeological evidence that taxation existed in this country and that it posed a major problem for Pharaoh's subjects.

There is documented evidence that every two years, a biennial event took place that personally involved the Pharaoh traveling the country. This royal tour was called the "Following of Horus." The Egyptian leader would appear in front of his subjects to collect revenue that was due to him, because of his indisputable role as head of state. The Pharaoh was seen as the incarnation of Horus. Because of this divine role, all subjects of lesser status were obligated to pay a tribute.

Every year Egyptian subjects were required by law to pay excessive taxes on almost everything worthwhile they possessed. For example, they would have to make payments on the cattle, cooking oil, grain, and property they owned. As well, heavy taxes were imposed on the income of their profession or labor.

There was even the possibility of an ad hoc tax, where at any time the Pharaoh could demand taxes paid immediately to the scribes, an Egyptian tax collector, for military campaigns or work and materials for royal tombs.

Though most subjects in Ancient Egypt thought taxes were a burden, there is a letter from a priest of the New Kingdom who protested excessive taxes by writing, "It is not my due tax at all!" He may have been history's first recorded tax protester.

Ancient Greece

In Ancient Greece, direct taxation of income and wealth was never well–developed. There was a special tax called the *eisphora*, which was generally reserved for the very wealthy. However, in times of war, when military campaigns were deemed absolutely necessary to defend the country, the *eisphora* tax was levied on all households.

Liturgies were also imposed on large fortunes of the very rich. The money derived from the *liturgies* went to various social purposes or community constructions. The money could be used on any number of Greek projects, like a trireme, a chorus for a theater festival, or the construction of a new gymnasium. In many cases, the rich citizens of the nation were solicited for voluntary donations. At other times, there was a mandatory donation for outfitting and commanding a trireme.

Indirect taxes were more developed and imposed on a variety of excise items and properties. Publicans levied a tax on houses, land, property, slaves, herds and flocks, wines, and animal feed such as hay. These were but a few of the indirect taxes required from all Greek citizens.

Also, Athenians imposed a one–drachma monthly poll tax on foreigners. If you were not born of an Athenian mother and father, you were considered a foreigner, and obligated to pay the poll tax. This tax was known as *metoikion*, and only applied to foreigners living in Athens.

Roman Empire

The earliest known tax in Ancient Rome was called *portoria*. A tax imposed on customs duties for both imports and exports.

Caesar Augustus would be considered a great tax strategist by tyrants and fascist dictators, because he was able to develop a well–functioning tax collection system. During his reign, he practically eliminated the publicans as tax collectors. Instead of the central government collecting taxes, the cities were responsible to collect from their local citizens.

Caesar imposed an inheritance tax to provide retirement funds for the military. Retired militants, who protected their country and waged war on other nations, received a substantial amount of income after their military service. This example shows how a nation robs from ordinary citizens to give to a select group; a transfer of wealth from the majority to a minority.

Caesar Augustus, a "First Citizen" of Rome, followed closely in the footsteps of Julius Caesar. However, he made a few minor deviations. He taxed slaves a full 4% on all their labor and everything they possessed, if they owned anything at all. Secondly, he charged a 1% tax on everything, including the income on labor. Whereas, Julius Caesar had only imposed a 1% sales tax on exchanged goods and property.

Queen Boadicea from East Anglia started a revolution attributed to the corrupt tax collectors in the British Isles. In 60 ADE, the revolt she led killed all Roman soldiers within a 100 mile radius. Her revolutionary resistance movement was able to seize London. It is reported 80,000 Roman soldiers were massacred during her revolt. Those 80,000 soldiers faced an unexpected army of 230,000 armed tax resisters.

However, the Roman Emperor Nero crushed the revolutionists' uproar. Nero's campaign of conquer resulted in the appointment of a new administration in the British Isles.

<u>Great Britain</u>

The first tax imposed on the British Isles was during Roman occupation. When Rome fell, Saxon kings continued to impose taxes. These taxes were referred to as *danegeld*. The kings levied the *danegeld* on land and property. As well, the Saxons imposed heavy customs duties on imported and exported goods.

Thereafter, British citizens were continually taxed generation after generation. It was not until after the 1377 Poll Tax that income taxation became progressive for the British nation. Thereafter, those who were poor paid very little or no taxes. As a Britain annually earned more money from labor, sales, or investments, the higher the levied rate became. This was one of the first *progressive* tax schemes.

King Charles I was severely opposed for his views and practices of levying high taxes and his belief in the Divine Right of Kings. He fought with Parliament over these issues which ultimately led to his death on March 27th, 1625. He was charged with treason by Parliament, then executed.

In 1643, Parliament imposed an excise tax on essential commodities like grain, meat, and dairy to name a few. This tax funded the army commanded by Oliver Cromwell. These excise taxes raised more funds than those imposed during the leadership of King Charles I. Even the poor were indirectly taxed, because whatever they needed to live and survive carried a built–in tax. This kind of tax was considered regressive by the citizens, including the poor, and led to the Smithfield riots in 1647.

Throughout the past 5,000 years there has always been a king, ruler, leader, dictator, or governmental body that has sanctioned the collection of taxes through legally authorized theft. History also reveals there have been countless tax protesters and resisters, all with a single goal of retaining their physical and financial freedom.

In the next chapter, we will closely examine the foundation of the United States by taking a close look at Colonial America to understand the revolt behind the Revolutionary War, and gain a new appreciation for the Founding Fathers of America.

A New World

During the period of the Revolutionary War (1775–1783) a new world was born in North America. This revolution was also known as the American War of Independence. It was when the thirteen colonies of America went head–to–head against the British Empire over taxes.

The true origins of the American Revolution are usually glossed over in the history books of public schools. Most Americans are familiar with the basic details. However, let us refresh our memories and see why the revolution occurred.

By 1763, the British Empire possessed a vast amount of land in North America. Besides the thirteen colonies, there existed twenty–two smaller colonies. These colonies were ruled directly by royal governors.

The British Empire was able to expand their ownership of land to include New France, Spanish Florida, and Native American lands east of the Mississippi River. Possession of this land was acquired by victory in the Seven Years' War (1756–1763) against the major European powers. To pay for the Seven Years' War the British government chose to tax its American possessions. This taxation against the colonists was enacted to fund the defense of North America.

After the Seven Years' War, most American colonists still considered themselves loyal subjects of Great Britain. They maintained the same rights and obligations as subjects residing in the British Isles with the exception of the taxes they were required to pay.

In 1764, British Parliament enacted the Sugar Act and Currency Act, which further vexed the colonists. Most American colonists had a problem with these new taxes imposed upon them. Their debate was with the premise and obligation forced upon them.

It was not until 1765 when the Stamp Act was levied that all thirteen colonies vehemently protested. Popular leaders of these protesters included Patrick Henry of Virginia and James Otis of Massachusetts. They were able to rally the people in wildly passionate opposition against the British Empire and their "taxation without representation." In many towns, secret groups known as the "Sons of Liberty" were formed. Their sole purpose was to threaten anyone selling the British stamps, with violence if necessary. Their protesting efforts met with great success reducing the Crown's revenues.

On March 5, 1770, British troops killed seven American colonists. This was the consequence of a large mob that surrounded British soldiers. Everything was fine until a soldier opened fire on the crowd and others followed suit, hitting eleven civilians at the scene and killing five. Two more colonists died later. Word about the killings quickly spread throughout Boston and the other colonies. Descriptions of the Boston Massacre were exaggerated and began a downward spiral in the relationship between Britain and the colonies. Massachusetts showed the greatest degree of antipathy toward Britain after the incident.

On Thursday, December 16, 1773, the Sons of Liberty led by Samuel Adams disguised themselves as Narragansett and Mohawk Indians and boarded the ships of British tea merchants. They took direct action to hurl large crates of tea overboard into the Boston Harbor, destroying an estimated £10,000 worth of tea. This single act of rebellion was prompted by their disgust with the Stamp Act of 1765 and the Townshend Act of 1767. Tea continued to wash up on the shores around Boston for weeks.

The Boston Tea Party and other similar acts of rebellion proved to be the necessary catalyst to begin the Revolutionary War.

On April 19, 1775, a British regiment was sent to seize arms and arrest revolutionaries in Concord, Massachusetts. This later became known as the Battle of Lexington and Concord when revolutionaries opposed the British government and soldiers and began fighting. News quickly spread and militias from all colonies were prepared to fight a bloody war.

The war lasted for eight years until 1783. However, in 1776 the colonists declared their independence from British power. The Second Continental Congress declared on July 4, 1776 that the colonies in North America were a "free and independent state" and "all political connection between them and the State of Great Britain, is and ought to be totally dissolved." The document explained the justifications for separation.

John Hancock, as elected President of Congress, was the only individual to sign the Declaration of Independence on July 4th. On August 2, 1776, the other fifty–five delegates signed the freedom document. These fifty–five individuals, along with John Adams of Massachusetts, Benjamin Franklin of Pennsylvania, and Thomas Jefferson of Virginia, are considered the Founding Fathers of the United States.

What these noble men did, along with the countless militants and colonists, was protest against an oppressive monarchist government that imposed taxes on labor and goods. The colonists said they were not willing to take anymore and revolted, causing a war that ensured their right to freedom, happiness, and wealth. The Founding Fathers caused a new world to be born.

After the United States made and earned their independence, there was only a federal income tax on two brief occasions before 1913. The majority of those 124 years were absent of taxation on labor and wages[1].

---

[1] A federal income tax was levied by Congress in 1861 and later repealed in 1872. Again, a federal income tax on wages was enacted in 1894, but struck down by the U.S. Supreme Court case Pollock v. Farmers' Loan and Trust Co., 157 U.S. 428. Before 1913, these were the only two incidents of taxation in the first 124 years of American history.

Evils of a Centralized Bank

Today, as I write this chapter, the national debt of the United States of America is over $9.3 trillion[1]. Since September 26, 2006, the debt of the U.S. has increased on average at $1.56 billion per day. With an estimated population of 304 million people, each man, woman and child's share of that ludicrous debt is approximately $31,000. Thomas Jefferson, one of the Founding Fathers of the new world, had this to say about a nation's debt:

> *"I place economy among the first and most important virtues, and public debt as the greatest of dangers. To preserve our independence, we must not let our rulers load us with perpetual debt." – Letter to William Plumer, 1816*

Unless the debt is paid off immediately, then it will continue to compound and this financial and economic mess it creates shall remain perpetual. Thomas Jefferson was giving an experienced

---

[1] The dollar amount for the United States National Debt referenced in this book was calculated in March 2008.

warning, since he personally witnessed the tragedy of debt and interest in his day. National debt, owed to bankers who are cloaked in
mystery and deceit, is a dangerous thing for any country. For us to
fully understand the severity the United States now faces, we must
take a look back into history, even before our country was born, at
other centralized banking systems and devious money swindlers.

The system of private banking, later used by the same Moneychangers of the Ancient Jewish Temple, could be said to start during the reign of King Kandalanu of Babylon (648–625 BCE). During the Israelite's captivity in Babylon, there arose a businessman
named Jacob Egibi who became the founding father of modern
banking. Jacob had a well–functioning banking system where he
would lend out money and collect large amounts of interest from
those debts. During those years of Israel's captivity, the Egibi family mentored other notable businessmen in the practice of private
banking and art of lending money at a high interest rate.

Before and after the trial, crucifixion, and resurrection of Jesus the Christ, private banking continued to flourish in the Roman
Empire, Egypt, and Arab nations of the Red Sea. Though Jesus
strictly and dramatically opposed taxation and the cunning private
banking system, he was not able to single–handily put these men
out of business. Immediately after Jesus' crucifixion, the Jewish
Moneychangers congregated in the Jewish Temple and were running their money lending business again. This time without the
threat or harassment of the Rabbi revolutionist.

Private banking was adopted in Europe and continued until the Renaissance period. A few European kings despised usury or charging interest on money lent. Alfred the Great (849–901), King of England, made this statement in opposition to usury:

> *"If a man is found taking usury, his lands will be confiscated, and he will be banished from England."*

King James I of England (1566–1625) further elaborated on what Alfred the Great had said. Here is what King James I said about collecting interest on the practice of lending money:

> *"If a man is found taking usury, his lands will be confiscated. It is like taking a man's life, and it must not be tolerated."*

In 1694, King William III and his administration were struggling financially. They desperately needed money to run the daily royal affairs and country. Word quickly spread and William Patterson united the wealthiest men in England together. Patterson presented the idea of loaning money to the King's government. The King gladly accepted the 1,200,000 pounds at 8% interest.

Also, the government of England granted Patterson and his associates a charter to form a centralized bank for the country. They called it the Bank of England and were allowed to produce and issue bank notes under exclusive rights granted by the King of England.

Whenever the government needed more money, the Bank of England literally produced money out of nothing, printing paper notes at the request of the King. This is the exact method the Federal Reserve employs in modern America. A dangerous practice for any government and for the citizens of that nation.

In 1773, Germany and the world saw the birth of the Rothschild empire. Mayer Amschel Bauer (1743–1812), a wealthy goldsmith and coin dealer by trade, summoned twelve of the wealthiest and most influential men to his shop in Frankfurt, Germany. He outlined a 25–point[2] plan on how to obtain control of the world's wealth, its natural resources, and its manpower. Along with Adam Weishaupt, the founder of the Illuminati, a plan was outlined to obtain control of the world's financial markets and governments through deception, vice, influence, and manipulation.

Soon thereafter, Bauer changed his surname to Rothschild, meaning "red sign." On the outside of his shop, there was a red sign with an eagle clutching five arrows. A symbol he said represented himself and his five sons.

Rothschild later mentored his five sons in the practice of lending money, charging high interest, and the 25–point system he devised. When the sons were mature in age and knowledge, he dispatched each son to a different city in Europe. Each son established a branch of the Rothschild banking firm. The most notable son was

---

[2]The Rothschild's 25–point plan mentioned in this chapter can be located in the Appendix. The same 25–point plan was also discovered in Illuminati communications and documents.

Nathan Mayer who took control of the Bank of England.

This is what Nathan Mayer Rothschild had to say about taking control of England's money supply:

> *"I care not what puppet is placed upon the throne of England to rule the Empire on which the sun never sets. The man who controls Britain's supply controls the British Empire, and I control the British money supply." – 1820*

In 1850, after William Patterson lost control of the Bank of England, the House of Rothschild controlled and dominated more wealth than all the families of Europe.

When the new world of the United States was born, the colonists won their political freedom but their financial independence was in severe jeopardy. The international bankers controlled by the Rothschild family had a secret agent in the midst of the American people. His name was Alexander Hamilton[3]. He married into the Rothschild family on December 14, 1780 by wedding Elizabeth Schuyler. Hamilton was surely a great political thinker. Unfortunately, he pushed for a central bank. Thomas Jefferson

---

[3] Alexander Hamilton was an Army officer, lawyer, statesman, financier, and political theorist. He was the first Secretary of the Treasury from September 11, 1789 to January 31, 1795. Hamilton is responsible for co–authoring the *Federalist Papers*.

passionately lobbied in opposition to Hamilton's central bank. Jefferson argued it was unconstitutional to form a centralized banking system.

The international bankers formed a central bank in 1781 and it was known as the Bank of North America. However, nine years later, in 1790 the bank closed operations due to pressure from the Americans. They saw that it was mirrored after the Bank of England and wanted to have nothing to do with it.

As quickly as the bank closed, the international moneychangers gained a charter for a new financial institution on February 25, 1791. It was called the Bank of the United States.

The bank's charter was to expire in 1836. Andrew Jackson, a presidential candidate at that time, was the first political candidate to publicly campaign in the United States. He campaigned strongly against the central bank, gaining the support of Americans for his candidacy and their opposition to the central bank.

He rallied the people with his public speeches. In 1828, a passionate Jackson said to a group of investment bankers:

> *"You are a den of vipers. I intend to wipe you out, and by the Eternal God I will rout you out. If people only understood the rank injustice of the money and banking system, there would be a revolution by morning."*

In 1836, the Bank of the United States lost its charter. Though the bank was closed, the international bankers did not lose their influence on America, nor in the rest of the world. They continued to dominate and influence. Money goes far and speaks an influential language to the greedy and immoral.

In 1913, the Federal Reserve Act was enacted by Congress and signed by President Woodrow Wilson. The United States again had a central bank. The third time it took form as the Federal Reserve, which incorporated in 1914.

It is interesting to note the Sixteenth Amendment to the United States Constitution was illegally ratified in 1913, the same year the Federal Reserve Act passed Congress. Certainly, the international moneychangers along with select dirty politicians were enacting plans to plunge the country and American people into a national debt and crisis.

President James Garfield realized the inevitable dangers of centralized banks:

> *"It must be realized that whoever controls the volume of money in any country is absolutely master of all industry commerce."*

The Federal Reserve was able to bankrupt America within 25 years. This happened in 1938 due to the inherent dangers of having a centralized banking system. The Founding Fathers would have been appalled with the Federal Reserve, then and now.

Dr. Ron Paul, a Texas Congressman and Presidential hopeful, clearly perceives the economic problem with centralized banking and its print–to–spend scheme. In an article titled, *Government Spending—A Tax on the Middle Class*, he states:

"Paying for government spending with Federal Reserve credit, instead of taxing or borrowing from the public, is anything but a good deal for everyone. In fact it is the most sinister seductive 'tax' of them all. Initially it is unfair to some, but dangerous to everyone in the end. It is especially harmful to the middle class, including lower–income working people who are thought not to be paying taxes.

"The 'tax' is paid when prices rise as the result of a depreciating dollar. Savers and those living on fixed or low incomes are hardest hit as the cost of living rises. Low and middle incomes families suffer the most as they struggle to make ends meet while wealth is literally transferred from the middle class to the wealthy."

Furthermore, Dr. Paul writes:

"The Fed is solely responsible for inflation by creating money out of thin air. It does so either to monetize federal debt, or in the process of economic planning through interest rate manipulation. This Fed intervention in our economy, though rarely even acknowledged by Congress, is more destructive than Members can imagine.

"Not only is the Fed directly responsible for inflation and economic downturns, it causes artificially low interest rates that serve the interests of big borrowers,

speculators, and banks. This unfairly steals income from frugal retirees who chose to save and place their funds in interest bearing instruments like CDs.

"The Fed's great power over the money supply, interest rates, the business cycle, unemployment, and inflation is wielded with essentially no Congressional oversight or understanding. The process of inflating our currency to pay for government debt indeed imposes a tax without legislative authority."

Another problem of the economy is fractional reserve banking. It can be properly defined as a system of banking in which banks are only required to hold a quantity of reserves that is a fixed fraction of the amount of money it creates. It is a common banking practice where a bank lends out more than it has in deposits or reserve. In the United States, fractional reserve banking is controlled and monitored by the Federal Reserve.

In an article titled, *Bush Establishes Financial Propaganda Council*, by Lee Rogers of Rogue Government, the author provides a recap of how the Federal Reserve and their method of fractional reserve banking has weakened the American and global economies:

The financial ups and downs that we see is a direct result of the fractional reserve banking system which uses a monetary unit that has no tangible backing by gold, silver or any other hard asset. During the 19th century, the United States saw great economic expansion because we had a stable monetary system. Gold and silver was primarily used as money during this time. This encouraged savings because the money stored value. Inflation was non–existent throughout the 19th century with the exception of the Civil War when Lincoln issued Greenbacks to fund the war. After the formation of the Federal Reserve in 1913, the bankers sought to destroy the link between the monetary system and gold. They were able to do that after engineering the Great Depression by intentionally putting a squeeze on the money supply. This is why there was a massive deflation during this time period. They used the economic problems that they created in order to justify a seizure of the gold using the excuse that it would help solidify the economy. The gold was melted down and taken to Fort Knox, KY. Ownership of gold in any substantive quantity was made illegal domestically. This ended the gold standard from a domestic standpoint. Internationally, gold was still accepted for the U.S. Dollar until 1971 when Richard Nixon shut the window on gold redemption and ended the post World War II Bretton Woods agreement which had made the U.S. Dollar the world's reserve currency. The Federal Reserve had printed too much money and there wasn't enough gold to be exchanged for the amount of Dollars they created. Since that point in time, the Federal Reserve has literally printed the money out of thin air, created all of the economic booms and busts through the manipulation of interest rates and the money supply. They have devalued the U.S. Dollar by over 95% since 1913 which slowly robbed wealth from the American people through their creation of additional Dollars otherwise known as inflation. It is a simple supply and demand issue, and right now the Federal Reserve has created too many Dollars which is causing massive inflation and currency devaluation. The mortgage meltdown and the fiasco in the global stock markets the past couple of days are a symptom of the irresponsible and downright criminal monetary policies of the Federal Reserve.

Now we have an economic recession and a foreshadowed depression because of the pressing actions of our government and the international bankers. Not only is the American nation threatened with depression, so is the global economy.

The moneychangers are no different than they were in the times of Jesus. However, our breed of vultures are more dangerous and willing to do anything to make sure they keep the wealth they stole from their innocent, and sometimes, naive victims.

The U.S. Constitution and Taxes

With the foreign bankers setting up their financial empire in the United States via the means of a centralized bank, they have been able to siphon, with very little notice, trillions of dollars from the American public. Though the Federal Reserve was incorporated in 1914 as the official bank of the United States, it has never been operated or maintained by the federal government. Even though the U.S. President "officially" appoints a chairman to the Federal Reserve, this is only done as a public gesture in recognition of the spokesperson the Federal Reserve selects. The authority is indirect, but compelling, for the President appoints and the Senate confirm who shall serve on the Federal Reserve board.

In a federal cost report delivered to President Ronald Reagan on January 12, 1984, the Grace Commission accounted for federal government spending and taxation. Page 12 of the President's Private Sector Survey on Cost Control stated:

Resistance to additional income taxes would be even more widespread if people were aware that:

- *One–third of all their taxes is consumed by waste and inefficiency in the Federal Government as we identified in our survey.*

- *Another one–third of all their taxes escapes collection from others as the underground economy blossoms in direct proportion to tax increases and places even more pressure on law abiding taxpayers, promoting still more underground economy—a vicious cycle that must be broken.*

- *With two–thirds of everyone's personal income taxes wasted or not collected, 100 percent of what is collected is absorbed solely by interest on the Federal debt and by Federal Government contributions to transfer payments. In other words, all individual income tax revenues are gone before one nickel is spent on the services which taxpayers expect from their Government.*

What the report to President Reagan claimed is that every single tax dollar sent to the U.S. Treasury is redirected and deposited into the Federal Reserve coffers. The money from American taxpayers never goes to the federal government. The international bankers steal every last cent.

How is this done? And how do the corrupt bankers get away with it?

Prior to 1913 when the Revenue Act passed Congress and the Sixteenth Amendment was illegally ratified by Secretary of State Philander Chase Knox, there existed no federally imposed income tax on personally earned wages. Less than twenty states legally ratified the amendment by following their own state–level constitutions and receiving the necessary votes from their state legislature. Woodrow Wilson hand–picked Philander Knox as Secretary of State. Knox was in a hurry to pass the Sixteenth Amendment, because the textual language of the amendment could be used to manipulate naive American minds. There were numerous versions suggested, but Knox and the New World Order were particular to the "ratified" reading.

The text of the Sixteenth Amendment reads:

> *"The Congress shall have power to lay and collect taxes on incomes, from whatever source derived, without apportionment among the several States, and without regard to any census or enumeration."*

This amendment was passed into law by Secretary of State Knox on February 25, 1913. Later that year, on October 3, 1913, President Wilson signed the Revenue Act of 1913 into law. The Revenue Act allowed for the first federal income tax to be imposed on American citizens. The U.S government in every subsequent decade provided several revisions to the Revenue Act, which would alter the taxes, graduation of rates, and additional measures the government needed to ensure a steady flow of increasing revenues.

Upon first reading the Sixteenth Amendment, it appears the federal government has every right to impose and collect taxes on incomes without consulting the states or conducting a census. Of course it would seem this way. Most people do not understand how the framers of the Constitution or Supreme Court defined the word income. In early federal court cases, the Supreme Court clearly defined income.

The Supreme Court of the United States officially defined income as:

"Income is the gain derived from capital, from labor, or from both combined including the profit gained through a sale or conversion of capital assets."

Additionally, Merriam–Webster's Dictionary of Law defines income as:

"...a gain or recurrent benefit usually measured in money that derives from capital or labor; also: the amount of such gain received in a period of time."

When a worker earns money from labor, that person is trading his time, energy, skills, talents, and work for a predetermined monetary substitute. The willingness of the employer and worker is an agreement to trade productive work for money. It is a trade;

nothing is gained. So, according to the Supreme Court, money derived from work is not income. A gain results when hired labor combines with invested capital to produce a net profit.

From re–reading the Sixteenth Amendment with this knowledge passed down from the Supreme Court, it would appear the amendment would apply to corporations and businesses who make a profit from the sale of their goods and services.

However, in 1920, the Supreme Court, deciding on the Mark Eisner vs Myrtle H. Macomber case, clearly stated the Sixteenth Amendment had no power that was not already defined in the U.S. Constitution. The Court stated:

> *"The Sixteenth Amendment must be construed in connection with the taxing clauses of the original Constitution and the effect attributed to them before the Amendment was adopted."*

The Court decided the Sixteenth Amendment did not give any new powers to the federal government that it did not have before. The United States could not directly collect an income tax prior to 1913, nor does it have the power to collect a federal income tax today.

This is what the U.S. Constitution states in Section 8 about direct taxes (i.e. federal income tax):

*"No Capitation, or other direct, Tax shall be laid, un-
less in Proportion to the Census or Enumeration herein
before directed to be taken."*

It also indicates in Section 8 that taxes must be "uniform throughout the United States" and only collected for the "common Defence and general Welfare of the United States." The money collected from the citizens under the guise of a federal income tax is not used for either, but strictly collected for repaying the debt of borrowed money. Furthermore, offensive wars, such as the recent wars in Afghanistan and Iraq, have not defended the freedoms of the United States, but were used to conquer foreign nations for oil, political reasons, and other purposes. General welfare is not endless social programs for citizens, but the maintenance of a healthy government to ensure ethical laws and uphold those laws in light of the U.S. Constitution.

But consider the fact that the U.S. Constitution, which once approved of slavery, continues to sanction taxation without limit.

Black Hand: American Style

As mentioned in the first chapter, the Internal Revenue Service, formerly known as the Bureau of Internal Revenue, is the powerfully secretive extortion racket of the United States government. The federal government, which is in the business of operating an unlawful and unethical crime syndicate, uses the IRS like the Mafia. It enables the Black Hand to extort money from innocent victims. Since the federal government has a long–standing agreement with the international moneychangers for lending and producing new money, it is necessary to have an enforceable method of collecting revenue to pay the accrued interest stipulated and required by the foreign bankers.

The methods employed by the IRS for collection of unpaid and back taxes is abusive. There are countless incidents of abuse on American citizens, some reports that never see the light of day. A prepared statement of a witness for a Senate Finance Committee hearing indicate a grave situation:

> "Does the IRS correct abuses when they become aware of them? Oftentimes, they do. However, the more im-

portant question is, does the IRS cover up occurrences of abuse? The answer is, yes! If the true number of incidences of taxpayer abuse were ever known, the public would be appalled. If the public also ever knew the number of abuses covered up' by the IRS, there could be a tax revolt."

If enough people awaken to the truth, America will see a tax revolt. There are many reasons, besides constitutional violations previously stated, that a revolution should happen. Criminal Investigation Special Agents, working as sworn law enforcement officers, have notoriously been reported by citizens for their unethical practices of harassment, intimidation, persecution, slander, lying, physical assaults, and unwarranted seizure of person and property. Agents have been known to arrest citizens without a warrant and bring charges against them for tax evasion. These agents blatantly violate clauses of constitutional law.

IRS Special Agents have even taken to undercover work, in an effort to entrap business owners looking to sell their business to prospective buyers. These IRS Special Agents produce fake business cards and pretend to be a business broker, clergyman, lawyer, used car salesmen, or any number of professions, attempting to lure in potential sellers. The U.S. Court of Appeals, in the United States vs. Centennial Builders case, sided with the corrupt and deceptive practices of the IRS. They made the following decision:

"In the end, the appellant's arguments boiled down to

the proposition that it is just not fair for an undercover IRS agent to entice taxpayers into discussing assets relating to their tax liability without informing them of his identity as an IRS Agent. We have rejected similar contentions before and we reject them here. We are not here to prescribe 'fair' rules for the 'game' of lawmen vs. lawbreaker. The law does not denounce clever or innovative police work within the bounds of the Constitution even though the lawbreaker really has no chance of escaping prosecution."

The ruling judges on this appeals case must have been crazy. How can they even call themselves judges when they rule in favor of unconstitutional police practices and insist they are constitutional? Their judgment violates the clause of apportionment on direct taxation covered under Section 8 of the U.S. Constitution and the Fourth Amendment when a federal representative must describe "the place to be searched, and the person or things to be seized."

The IRS through abuse, corruption, and entrapment strikes fear into the heart of Americans. Special Agents from the Criminal Investigation Division could show up at your home or place of work any day, intimidate you, seize your property and financial documents, and arrest you in front of onlookers like your loved ones or co–workers. To top off this embarrassing and personally degrading situation, the IRS could hold you without bail. After your arrest, two Special Agents could interrogate you for hours disregarding and disrespecting your rights. Weeks or months later, you could find yourself on trial in one of the lower courts for tax evasion or any number of trumped up charges often including a felony conspiracy charge.

The authority of the Internal Revenue Service is immense and intrusive. The IRS violates privacy and property rights, in order to make examples of non–taxpayers. Tax resisters and non–taxpayers are scrutinized and abused by this federal agency more times than taxpayers. Those who pay their taxes willingly and without coercion are no threat to the IRS. It is when citizens stop paying their taxes or misrepresent information on their tax return forms that they draw attention. Compliance is never a threat; non–compliance brings suspicion, investigation, and intrusive action.

Even as a taxpayer, the Internal Revenue Service never has your best interest in mind. Their only concern is to collect and enforce the system of taxation. There are over 100,000 employees nationwide working to process collections and ensure a continual flow of payments into the U.S. Treasury, awaiting its transfer to the Federal Reserve bank. Work life for IRS employees has drastically improved. In 1943, less than 1% of U.S. citizens even paid a federal tax. For decades, the IRS relied on the honor system; citizens would mail in payments yearly. In our modern age, the IRS utilizes the latest technology to its fullest benefit and employs the illegal method of tax withholding at the employer–level.

Employers are required by Internal Revenue Code 3401 to withhold a portion of their employee's paycheck and send that amount to the U.S. Treasury. This method of collection has resulted in tremendous results for the IRS. Most employees do not have the ability to opt–out of federal tax withholding. Though it is unconstitutional in multiple ways to require a new or existing employee to file a W–4 form, an employee who does not comply with this procedure will not receive employment or be fired for violating this IRS requirement. The IRS, assisted by employers throughout the United States, make it difficult for a person to maintain a stable livelihood without compliance. They make it almost impossible to escape taxes.

The only possible way to overcome this mandatory taxation system is non–violent resistance. Even unto the point of a tax revolt.

How Citizens Are Negatively Affected

I urge everyone to resist paying taxes in a non–violent way. Government, along with their system of taxation, is the spawn of the devil. Any ruler who reigns besides the sovereign individual united with God is a ruler who will eventually lead the people astray. The Lord's voice in 1 Samuel 8:11–20 provides a warning for all generations of the earth:

> *And he said, This will be the manner of the king that shall reign over you: He will take your sons, and appoint them for himself, for his chariots, and to be his horsemen; and some shall run before his chariots.*
>
> *And he will appoint him captains over thousands, and captains over fifties; and will set them to ear his ground, and to reap his harvest, and to make his instruments of war, and instruments of his chariots.*
>
> *And he will take your daughters to be confectionaries, and to be cooks, and to be bakers.*

And he will take your fields, and your vineyards, and your oliveyards, even the best of them, and give them to his servants.

And he will take the tenth of your seed, and of your vineyards, and give to his officers, and to his servants.

And he will take your menservants, and your maidservants, and your goodliest young men, and your asses, and put them to his work.

He will take the tenth of your sheep: and ye shall be his servants.

And ye shall cry out in that day because of your king which ye shall have chosen you; and the LORD will not hear you in that day.

Nevertheless the people refused to obey the voice of Samuel; and they said, Nay; but we will have a king over us;

That we also may be like all the nations; and that our king may judge us, and go out before us, and fight our battles.

Allow me to share a few stories to illustrate how counterproductive and treacherous the system of taxation is to the American economy.

The first story is of a woman in her mid–forties. As a matter of privacy, I will not disclose her real name. For a matter of reference, I shall use Jamie.

Jamie has two children, both grown men, who currently live with her. Her boys recently became unemployed. As a good mother, she continues to take care of them and allows them to live under her roof. Since Jamie is not married and cannot claim her children on her tax return, she is unable to write them off.

Jamie works full–time. Not only that, she works over twenty hours overtime per week. Though it can be very physically taxing on her body, she finds great enjoyment and satisfaction in the work she does. She is one of the most passionate workers I have known.

In 2007, she earned over $58,000 in wages for all her hard work and dedication. One day she was sharing in confidence about her tax returns and what percentage the federal government garnishes on her wages. When she told me she falls into the twenty–five percent graduation, my mouth almost dropped to the floor. That is an ungodly amount for a mother providing for her two grown children. That twenty–five percent does not include Social Security, Medicare, and state income taxes. I was appalled! This hard–working mother only gets to keep fifty percent of her wages.

Our next story is of a hard–working father. His name is David. He has five children, one of them a newborn baby. His wife stays home all day to watch the kids and provide the necessary motherly love and guidance. While she stays home, David wakes up around three–thirty every morning to make it to a part–time job. This part–time job in a warehouse requires moving heavy boxes and merchandise all morning. When he is done with his first job, he takes a short break to eat something and then head off to his full–time job.

At his second job, David puts in fifty to sixty hour a week. He usually clocks out and leaves the building around nine p.m. He does not make it home to his lovely wife and beautiful children until ten o'clock. His time with his family is severely limited, because he has to find a few moments to relax before going to bed again. He has maintained this type of work life for a few years, just to support his family.

If it were not for a last–minute miracle, his family would not have enjoyed Christmas in December 2007. David told me they could not afford to buy groceries. When they received a generous gift of enough money, David and his wife were able to fill their car's gas tank, stock the kitchen with food, and purchase a few Christmas gifts for each of the children and themselves. Those tough times continue with David working all day.

David and his wife can write off each child and reduce their taxes because they are married. He told me when he files his 2007 tax return he expected to get back $12,000 of the amount withheld from his wages. That is $1,000 per month. If he had that $1,000 extra in his bank account each month, his financial situation would have been brighter.

How much more would he have if Americans did not pay taxes?

A substantial amount more. He would also be financially independent with his wife. If he had more money on each paycheck, he could get rid of his second job and spend more time with his family. One of the best benefits a father can have is spending quality time with his family.

The third story comes from Irwin Schiff[1], one of the leading tax experts in the tax resistance movement. The following excerpt from pages 225–227 of *The Great Income Tax Hoax* reads:

> *For example, take an employer and one of his own employees, say an electrical contractor and one of his electricians such as attended one of my recent tax seminars. I asked the employee, "Does he (pointing to his employer seated next to him) pay you wages?"*
>
> *"Yes he does," replied the electrician.*
>
> *"Are you worth what he pays you?" I asked.*
>
> *"I'm worth more." His answer–the standard one–evoked laughter from the audience.*
>
> *I then turned to his employer and said, "Is he really worth more than what you pay him?"*
>
> *Now the employer appeared perplexed since, if he said yes, he might be hit for an immediate raise. But finally*

---

[1] Irwin Schiff has written numerous books in support of the tax honesty movement. He has been wrongfully convicted of tax evasion a number of times. He is currently serving a 13-plus year sentence in prison and his projected release date is October 7th, 2016.

he good naturedly replied, "Yes, he is." The audience responded with more laughter.

Carrying this admission further, I asked, "In other words, Mr. Employer, your employee is worth a good deal more than what you are paying him, is that right?"

Once again the employer said yes and drew more laughter from the audience and a good natured reaction from his (admittedly) underpaid employee. I decided to take the pressure off the employer and said to the audience, "Of course his employee is worth more than he pays him. What would be the point of hiring him if he weren't?" And, looking at the employee, I said, "You better hope you're worth more than he's paying you. If you're not then he's overpaying you and his other employees, and he'll soon be broke and out of business and you'll be out of a job!"

Essentially companies are in business to make a profit by paying their employees less (collectively) than what they can sell their work–product for. If they cannot do that they will go out of business and their employees will be out of jobs.

Driving my point further I said to the employer, "In other words, Mr. Employer, you might bill a customer $40.00 an hour for your employee's time but pay the employee only $20 an hour, isn't that right?"

"Yes," he replied.

"Now," I continued, "I realize that some of that differential is to cover your overhead, but you still make a direct profit on his labor don't you?"

"Yes," he said, "I do."

"So, he gives you his labor, and you give him money which we'll call wages, is that correct?"

"Yes," he answered.

"You receive his labor and he receives your money—but, in any case, the labor you get from him is worth more than the money he gets from you. Is that correct?"

"Yes," he replied.

"Now," I asked the employee, "did you pay income taxes last year on the money he gave you?"

"Yes," answered the employee. Obviously this was his first seminar.

Turning once again to the employer I said, "Did you pay income taxes last year?"

"Yes," he answered. Obviously it was his first seminar, too.

"In the tax return you filed, did you include the value of the labor you received from him?"

With his eyes riveted to mine and a puzzled look on his face the employer replied, "I'm not sure I understand you."

"Look," I said, "you just admitted that your employee gave you his labor. Did you add the value of that labor—as indicated by his wages—to the income you reported for tax purposes?"

He hesitated before replying, "No."

"Then how did you show the value of the labor you received from him on your tax return?" I asked.

"Well, I took his wages as a tax deduction," he said.

"So, not only didn't you pay a penny of taxes on the labor you received from him but you actually reduced your own taxes by the amount of that labor, correct?"

"That's right," he said.

Turning back to the employee I said, "Did you hear what your employer just said? He said that not only didn't he pay taxes on what you gave him—your labor— but he actually paid less taxes because of it. You, however, told me a short while ago that you paid on what he gave you. Now we find out that what he got from you actually reduced his taxes. Does that make sense to you?"

"No, it doesn't," he replied.

*"Well, it doesn't make sense to me either. So why
don't you do what he does? If he deducts from his
income taxes the labor you give him, why don't you
deduct from your income tax the money he gives you?
In other words, since he deducts the value of your labor from his income, why don't you deduct the value
of his money from your income and treat his wages the
way he treats your labor. Then you wouldn't have any
income taxes to pay. Doesn't that make more sense
that what you're doing now?"*

"It certainly does," he replied.

*Can you see why the electrician had no "income"? He
had no "income" because he had no gain on his labor.
His employer admitted he paid him less for his labor
than what it was worth. As a matter of fact, not only
did the electrician not have a "gain" on the transaction,
he actually lost on the exchange!*

All three examples show how we lose money by giving it away
willingly to a cunning federal government.

For a moment, calculate in your head or on a piece of paper the
amount of taxes that reduce your paycheck. Figure out how much
is taken out monthly and yearly. Sit for a moment and examine
those numbers. What could you do with that extra money?

You could do whatever you like with that money. After all, that money rightfully belongs to you. That money was exchanged for your time and labor. Your labor cannot be separated from its source; you are the source of your work!

A Tax Free World

A tax revolt is inevitable. One day, whether in the United States, or in a foreign land with a different flag soaring high, a revolution against taxation is bound to happen. Imagine a country without taxes on wages, profits, customs, duties, excises, sales, or any other number of taxable items, goods, or services. The end of taxation is the end of big government meddling in our privates lives, stealing our rightfully owned property, and invading foreign nations for conquest, glory, and power.

Limited government[1] is the only way any nation can survive and maintain civil liberties, if government is actually necessary. It is possible to have inner freedom through spiritual means, but physical and financial independence only last if all people, including those who work for government, respect the boundaries of the sovereign individual. When a violation is made, the witnesses must speak up and testify against immoral behavior. Solutions

---

[1]Limited government has its roots in Hebraic Law, the Magna Carta, the United States Constitution, and the Bill of Rights. These are key examples of citizens limiting the powers of government.

must be proposed to offer corrective reform and guidance back to ethical principles. Every individual must discover and retain their sovereignty individually, but collectively they must transcend oppressive struggles and fearful inaction to ensure civil liberties for future generations.

If every person respected every other person, our world would definitely be a better place. To paraphrase the words of Mahatma Gandhi, *if we take an eye for an eye we will make the whole world blind*[2]. Civil violations provoked by more violent injustice and human vengeance only breed further violations against humanity. One day, instead of living in freedom, we could be utterly blind to all truth.

Non–violent resistance is the only way to rise up against the powers that oppress humanity and cloak the truth. It is time to wake up and envision how our world should be.

Our world should be a tax free world. Enforced taxes, whether by fear, coercion, abuse, inflation or unjust punishment, in the strictest sense, is robbery. Theft is theft, no matter what you call it.

If no one on earth paid taxes, each person would have additional money that represents the true wealth of their being. Money can be a good indicator of one's value to society, but only if a person is honest and does not steal from another human being. If they do steal property from another, they have devalued that individ-

---

[2]Mohandas Karamchand Gandhi, deceased Indian political activist and spiritual leader, is attributed with saying, *"An eye for an eye, and soon the whole world is blind."*

ual by the amount stolen. It is time to stand up for ourselves and neighbors and stop letting our governments rob us blind.

Tax cuts can improve a nation's economic condition, but no taxes would ensure the most liquid market of trade and exchange in the world. Prices for goods and services would be lower in a tax free world, because taxes accrued by businesses and corporations raise the cost and retail value. Paying less for the necessities and luxuries of life keeps more money in the pocket of working–class consumers. Laborers would earn higher wages in trade for their time and work. An increase in wages occurs for the same reason a product cost decreases; no taxes for the businesses that employ people and sell goods. A world without taxation inspires a free market and well–functioning economy.

A world without taxes would minimize theft and violent crimes. The logic is when everyone has adequate resources to provide for themselves and their family, it is not necessary to take from others. With an improved economy in our envisioned world, respectfulness would increase abundantly. Violations of individual boundaries would be minimal, forgiveness easily given, and corrective reforms successfully undertaken.

The duty of limited government is to secure the general welfare of the country and to protect the freedoms of all citizens. It is not the job of government to provide social programs; that is the duty of kind–hearted people and charitable organizations serving the greater good. The economic problems of homelessness and the necessity of welfare programs would be minimal.

A true limited government does not have a singular leader but a communal democracy where every citizen's opinion matters. Not a democratic republic with a few elected officials, but a non–state of self–governance where equality reigns with God–given rights. A land of liberty in a tax free world.

Part Three

Appendix

No More Taxes

Here is the original article that inspired this book:

Any spiritual teacher that insists taxation of personal income and wages is necessary must be a criminally–minded con-man, naive and gullible, or completely uneducated about the history of taxation. A government that imposes a requirement to pay taxes by their citizens is a government that enslaves their people. In the mind of any free man, taxes equates to slavery.

In ancient times, when an empire or nation defeated tribes or other nations in war or battle, the winning nation would punish the losers. The punishment would often occur in degrading and abusing the captured women, mandatory requirement to work, and taxing the working people a percentage of their income.

The first known system of taxation was in Ancient Egypt between 3000–2800 BC, the first dynasty of the Old Kingdom. Ancient records document how the Pharaoh would travel Egypt every 2 years, collecting a percentage of revenues from the people.

Before this time in ancient civilization, human beings faced tribal governments with no enduring problem of taxation.

As an example of a high tax, medieval serfs of the Middle Ages paid 25% of their earnings to their landlords. In ancient Israel, any income over 10% was considered usury or taxable at a high interest. When the Romans took over and occupied the region of Judah and Israel, they began to punish the Jews through forced taxation. In the days of Jesus, there was hatred and disgust towards tax collectors, especially those of Jewish descent.

According to the Bible, Jesus, a mystical and prolific spiritual teacher, was charged for tax protesting crimes and inciting disobedience against the Roman oppressors and authorities. Luke 23:1–2 (NIV) explicitly states: Then the whole assembly rose and led him off to Pilate. And they began to accuse him, saying, "We have found this man subverting our nation. He opposes payment of taxes to Caesar and claims to be Christ, a king."

Even the most famous spiritual teacher known to humanity blatantly opposed taxation.

Thousands of years later the American Revolution began. Contrary to popular belief, the Colonists' did not revolt due to a tea tax. The British Monarchy was imposing a 3-5% income tax on the Colonists' earnings. The revolution consisted of killing, maiming, property destruction and expensive battles for eight years, but the bitter relations lasted decades. All of this destruction because the British Monarchy would not cease their practices of taxation and slavery.

After the new union was set apart from Britain, there was no individual income tax for 124 years. Except for two brief periods, during 1862–1872 (an "income duty" to pay for the Civil War) and 1874–1875 (until the Supreme Court declared it unconstitutional), the United States thrived without a national income tax imposed on its population. Americans were free to earn, save, spend, build, invest, and donate their money as they wished, without limitation, nor fear of taxation. The United States was able to support itself through tariffs on imports and exports, excise taxes on liquor, and by issuing government bonds.

To this day, the federal government of the United States of America, continues to tax the income of hard-working citizens. All states within the union, except seven (including Alaska, Florida, Nevada, South Dakota, Texas, Washington, and Wyoming), require a mandatory state income tax. In addition to the seven, there are two states (New Hampshire and Tennessee) that only tax dividends and earned interest on income[1].

The United States of America has been committing unconstitutional crimes of taxation and enslavement against its growing population (currently, 303 million citizens) since 1913.

If national income taxes were abolished, not only in the United States, but elsewhere, a nation's economy would thrive due to a free market of earning, spending, saving, and investing. Economic crisis would be a thing of the past while nations became more sta-

---

[1] All states in the Union tax their residents in one way or another. It could be a high property tax or a sales tax on goods and merchandise.

ble and free. People would have more money in their pocket to do with as they pleased. It would no longer be difficult to financially survive in this lifetime while feeding and sheltering one's family, loved ones, and self.

How can a government take from you what they do not own or have properly earned themselves? When you earn money through your skills, abilities, and strengths, you are the rightful owner of that income until you decide to spend or give that money to another person, business, or organization. Through a monetary system, the energy exerted and time spent working is converted into an adequate financial substitution. The money we earn is money that belongs to us; no man or government has the right to take it.

Do not give in helplessly subjecting yourself and your innately human rights to a government's whims and unnecessary spending. You are the people of your nation; in the highest reality, you are essentially free human beings.

Retain your freedom, defeat the system!

Interview with a Tax Protester

The following interview was conducted with Ned Netterville, author of *Jesus of Nazareth, Illegal Tax Protester* and an established tax protester in his own right:

1. When I wrote my first article about Jesus opposing government–sanctioned taxation, you were one of the first individuals, let alone authors who shared this similar knowledge about Jesus. When did you first realize or begin to study about Jesus' views of taxation?

I quit paying the federal income tax after having my return for 1971 audited by the IRS. The agent who audited my '71 return arbitrarily denied what I was certain was a legitimate business–expense. What's more, I felt I had proved the validity of the deduction to the satisfaction of any reasonable person. With penalties and interest, the agent's decision had the effect of increasing my tax for that year by a about $200. I was convinced that he had accessed me an amount which was just small enough to assure that I wouldn't contest his finding because to do so would cost me more (for the services of a lawyer I felt I would need) than paying the extra assessment. And I was convinced that the agent did so to compensate himself and his employer for the inordinate amount of time he had otherwise fruitlessly spent on the audit. So I paid, but my rather irrational response to the agent's "outrageous" behavior was to become what the IRS described as an "illegal tax protester." As a student of the Constitution, it seemed to me that the manner of enforcement of the income tax by the IRS conflicted with the Fourth and Fifth Amendments of the Constitution. It also appeared to me that people might be presumed to waive those rights by signing their income–tax return. Therefore, for the years 1976 through 1992, when I stopped filing altogether because it seemed redundant and a waste of time, I sent the IRS a signed copy of a 1040 tax return form with the following statement emblazoned across it: **I CANNOT PROVIDE THE INFORMATION REQUESTED HEREIN, UNLESS THE DEPARTMENT OF THE TREASURY WILL ENSURE ME THAT IN SO DOING ALL OF MY RIGHTS AS A CITIZEN OF THE UNITED STATES SHALL REMAIN INVIOLATE.** The Treasury never did provide me with any such assurance, and I have not provided the IRS with any information (or tax).

I think I have always objected to taxation as decidedly dishonest, and I have always been inclined to look askance on any authority. I did not believe the government could legally require its citizens to waive their constitutional rights in order to collect a tax. However, with that as background and more to the point of your question, in 1982 I underwent a transformation and spiritual awakening. My life at the time was fraught with personal problems and deteriorating relationships with my family and friends. Excessive drinking was the primary problem and it lay behind many of my other problems. I may have sensed that my real problem was essentially spiritual, for I began reading the Bible regularly, particularly the Gospels, in search of solutions. I was soon thereafter led, by God I believe, to join Alcoholics Anonymous, which enabled me to stop drinking. Following the example of the founders and other members of AA, I continued reading the Bible on a daily basis with new–found clarity of mind and more "sober" understanding. I concentrated on the New Testament and particularly on what Jesus reportedly said and did. I suppose it was through this repetitive pursuit of the Gospels combined with my deep–seated antipathy to taxes that I began to notice that references to taxes and tax collectors were ladled throughout the Gospels, beginning with Jesus' disparaging reference to tax collectors in his Sermon on the Mount. My ideas regarding Jesus' relationship to taxes and tax collectors developed gradually and progressively over a period of a decade or more. My studies broadened from the Bible to numerous other sources, all of which tended to confirm my growing belief that Jesus was as opposed to taxes as I was, and much more courageous in his opposition. My thoughts and beliefs were thereby pretty fully developed when I happened upon a book, an interpretation of the Gospels, which so egregiously twisted what Jesus had said and done regarding taxes I could scarcely restrain myself from attempting to debunk the author's distortions. However, when I sought confirmation of my views among other interpreters of the Gospels, I was astounded to discover that all of the "interpreter bibles" in the Cleveland Public Library (one of the 3 or 4 best general research libraries in the US with many such volumes) seemed to agree that Jesus had sanctioned taxes and the state. Since I knew better from my own studies of the Gospels, I set off to prove them all wrong. I should also mention that sometime, probably during the late '60, I became a political libertarian and read a great deal of libertarian oriented literature. I whole heartedly concurred in the libertarian position that taxation was theft because for the life of me I couldn't (and can't) see the distinction between extortion practiced by the state and that perpetrated by the Mafia. I finally sat down to write the essay that has become JESUS OF NAZARETH, etc., in 1995, or thereabouts. It only took me about 3 months to write the first draft, and I spend the next 8 years refining it while reading any confirming or conflicting literature I could find. I first "published" the essay on the Web in 2003 with the intention of soliciting criticism and then finalizing it within a year. That year has now stretched to 3 1/2, and I'm still not fully satisfied with it.

Given this background, some folks will say I used (or, they will say, misused) the Bible and twisted the words of Jesus to justify my own tax resistance. I suppose that is inevitable, and I won't waste time disputing such charges, which are beside the point. The essay, JESUS, etc., will ultimately be judged by the majority who peruse it on its merits rather than on my background. Furthermore, it is very unlikely that I would have ever noticed Jesus' opposition to taxes were it not for my own familiarity with many peculiarities and ramifications of taxation, which I acquired as a consequence of my personal experience as a tax resister. Living for as many years as I have under the constant possibility of prosecution and long–term imprisonment for "tax crimes" has made me sensitive and acutely aware of subtle nuances pertinent to taxation, which I do not think others may even notice. For this and other reasons, I consider my experience as a tax resister to be s a gift from God.

2. What is your formal or informal education in regards to economics, monetary systems, and taxation?

I have a BA in English. I minored in economics, which was one of the first scholarly disciplines I really enjoyed. I ended up graduating with many more hours in Economics than English. I subsequently studied economics as an avocation ever since I graduated in 1960. Reading The Freeman magazine during the late '60s introduced me to Ludwig von Mises. I've since read a fair amount of the the literature by economists belonging to the so–called Austrian school. I have definitely learned much more of economics informally than I did in school.

3. In the introduction of the essay, "Jesus of Nazareth, Illegal Tax–Protester", you briefly mentioned you were jailed for violation of man–made laws that conflict with your innately God–given rights. Would you mind elaborating on this?

I believe I have a right to travel by whatever means I choose without permission from the state. Licensing of any right by the state converts that right into a state–granted privilege. On the basis of this and my libertarian beliefs, in 1985 I let my driver's license expire permanently. Since then I have been stopped while driving by cops on several occasions, and in some of these instances the cop deemed it necessary to arrest me. In all of those cases I was

charged with the serious crime of "no operator's license," a.k.a.,
NOL. One judge was so incensed that I deemed it my right to drive
without the state's permission that he sentenced me to 90 days with
the proviso that I could avoid jail by obtaining a license. I couldn't
do that, so I did the time. Due to a paperwork snafu, I ended up
doing 97 days. It turned out to be a marvelous experience. I used
my time to study the New Testament, furthering my conviction that
Jesus didn't pay taxes. (Nor, by the way, did he apply to Rome for
any privilege.) Like a lot of prisoners do, I also worked out a lot. I
lost a huge amount of weight and left jail in the best physical condition I'd been in since I'd wrestled back in college. In fact I was in
such good shape that I took up mountain–bike racing that summer
(1998), and for the next six years raced almost every Sunday from
March through November—almost always as the oldest racer by
10 to 20 years. On several other occasions I spent from a day to a
week in jail for NOL. Also, in 1990 (I think it was.), I did 34 days
in jail as a ward of the federal government for "civil contempt," because I refused to comply with a federal judge's order that I comply
with an IRS "collection summons" of my tax records. Since civil
contempt lasts through eternity or until the victim complies, which
ever comes first, I got out after 34 days by promising to comply
because I wanted to spend Memorial Day with my family. I agreed
to give the IRS my records. Since I had no records, the IRS agents
were a bit disappointed, but by then they must have known they
couldn't get any money from me because I didn't have any. (As
I remember, the IRS was claiming I owed them something like a

quarter million $ or so.) I now think they then threw my file away and dismissed me as a pain–in–the–ass with no assets to steal, because I haven't been bothered by them since then.

4. Do you believe there to be errors in the translation of the Holy Bible? If so, what were your first encounters with this realization?

I do not believe that the Bible conveys the inerrant word of God. I believe that the authors in general were Divinely inspired, but their inspiration couldn't eliminate their susceptibility to err. Nor do I believe God enabled the translators and scribes of the Bible to do their work without error. Furthermore, as the works of the many scholars who have obviously misinterpreted Jesus' position on taxes clearly shows, anyone's and everyone's understanding of the meaning of the words written in the Bible is certain to be flawed to some extent because the Bible is a product of frail humans and the reader's comprehension of its meaning is equally imperfect.

5. Most Christians believe, *"Render unto Caesar the things which are Caesar's, and unto God the things that are God's,"* is Jesus' approval that citizens of a state or nation should subject themselves to government and pay their taxes. In short, why is this commonly–held viewpoint wrong?

The essay, JESUS OF NAZARETH, etc., answers this question at length, in depth, and in great detail. I don't think I can give you a short answer, because it was explicitly to answer this question that a long essay was written. However, try this: In short, the "common" view is wrong because it fails to logically analyze the situation and circumstances in which those words were uttered in light of everything else there is to know about Jesus from the Gospels, and, the view of most people has been greatly influenced by the misinterpretations of Christian–church exegetes beholden to the state and its taxes and thereby rendered unable to even consider that their Savior would condemn the state and its taxes upon which they depend—or, rather, think they depend, which is the same thing—for their welfare if not their very existence.

6. In your essay, you put forth the second hypothesis as being, *"Jesus taught and lived by principles diametrically opposed to government and taxes." How was this conclusion initially reached?*

The Gospels make it abundantly clear that Jesus professed and practiced nonviolence. The state and taxes are utterly dependent upon the initiation of force and violence. I cannot remember when I initially reached this obvious conclusion, but in retrospect it is as simple and transparent as one plus one equals two.

7. The third hypothesis from the essay makes claim that Pontius Pilate had Jesus executed for not being the "rightful" King of Israel, but because he was an illegal tax protester who taught taxation and its participation is ungodly. Would you please explain your reasoning for this conclusion? I believe

Christians of all faiths and sects, and taxpayers of all nations deserve a clear and reasonable explanation.

I believe the basis for the conclusion is made clear and reasonable in the essay. Perhaps it takes a little experience with resisting taxes to realize that those who are responsible for the collection of taxes, as Pilate was, cannot and do not tolerate resistance. This is so because any institution that requires the use of force for the fulfillment of its objectives rests on a precarious, unstable foundation. Those responsible for upholding the structure dare not let anyone shake the edifice. Jesus was killed for the very same reason that a runaway slave must be caught and publicly and severely punished. My analysis is based more on logic than on the Scriptures, as I explain in the essay. Would Pilate execute Jesus for publicly "forbidding us to pay taxes to Caesar," which is what his accusers accused him of doing? In a New–York minute they would. Pilate or any other tax administrator of a Roman–subjugated territory would do all withing his power to exterminate any sign of tax resistance, because the penalty for allowing tax resistance to foment and grow would be the end of any such administrator's tenure, and ultimately, if carried far enough, the end of the Empire. On the other hand, why would Pilate kill Jesus for calling himself king of the Jews? In the first place, Jesus never did call himself a king, and in the second place, even if he had done so it is illogical to suppose that doing so posed a threat to Pilate or to Rome. A king without an army would be as dangerous to Pilate and to Rome as a bow without arrows. Pilate consistently demonstrated such contempt for the one–time, long–ago Jewish "kingdom," that he would have found the charge ludicrous grounds for capital punishment.

8. From reading your essay and corresponding with you, it would seem you are a voluntaryist, if not by action, at least by principle. If this is true, how would you best define a voluntaryist?

I am indeed a voluntaryist, which I define as an anarchist, or in my case, as in the case of my voluntaryist mentor, Carl Watner, a pacifist anarchist. I understand that there are some voluntaryists who think the use of force is justified in self–defense, whereas, I do not think it is justified nor efficacious under any condition based on my understanding of the wisdom and ways of Jesus.

9. How is the ideology of a voluntaryist beneficial to oneself and society?

It is the most liberating ideology I can imagine. To quote a few passages from Carl Watner's essays compiled in his book, I MUST SPEAK OUT: "Voluntaryism offers a moral and practical way for advancing the cause of freedom. It rests on a belief in the efficacy of the free market and on a historic and philosophic antagonism to the State (and I would add, 'and its violence'). It rests on an understanding of the inter–relatedness of means and ends, and on a belief that 'if one takes care of the means, the end will take care of itself.' We are pro free market, anti–state, nonviolent and anti–electoral." It is personally liberating because, again to quote Carl,

"There is no guarantee that the voluntaryist method will be successful, but because each individual concentrates on himself and not others, it is worthwhile, profitable, and self–satisfying, even if it does not bring to fruition (its objective) in the short run or during one's life time." And quoting Edmund Quincy referring to the abolition movement in a 1841 editorial in The Non–Resistant (from Carl's book): "We would try to bring about a mightier revolution by persuading men to be satisfied to govern themselves according to the divine laws of their nature, and renounce [the attempt to govern others by] the laws of their own devising...We do not hold ourselves obliged to abandon the promulgation of what we believe to be truths because we cannot foretell how the revolution they are to work will go on, or what will be the form of the new condition they bring about...A reformer can have no plan but faith in his principles...We only know that truth is a sure guide, and will take care of us and of herself if we but follow her." In short, voluntaryism means: live and let live, which eliminates all the time, frustration, conflict and fruitless effort to control the behavior of others required by any system of humans governing humans.

10. How is taxation harmful to the individual?

Taxation is extortion, and extortion is theft. It corrupts and demolishes harmonious human relations in the same way stealing does. It harms both the collectors and recipients of taxes both morally and spiritually, just as stealing does. And it harms the taxpayer in the same way the victims of theft are harmed, perhaps even more so because there is no recourse or possible recovery of the loss of property to the tax collector. I think it also morally and spiritually harms taxpayers who, feeling or knowing it to be illicit, do not resist taxation. Harm is done to such taxpayers in the same way that voluntary compliance with extortion harms its victims. This is so because the person who docilely complies is virtually certain to join the rank of tax collectors (or tax receivers) at the earliest opportunity, and because paying an extortionist without protest or resistance emboldens and encourages further extortion.

11. How is taxation detrimental to society? And how does taxation negatively effect the economics of a state or nation?

In addition to corrupting the morals of society as explained above, taxation depletes the resources of society making everyone poorer. It does so because: A) Every project or action undertaken by means of taxation is perforce more costly than the corresponding project or action undertaken voluntarily because of the added costs of legislating, administering and enforcing the taxes to fund the project or action, costs that are not necessitated by voluntary actions or projects. B) Economic activity is either directed by the market or commanded by the state, which is to say it is either determined by the decisions of every member of society, or by the relatively few who elect and direct the state. Thus, government decisions are woefully uninformed of all the conditions, factors and circumstances at play in the project or activity as compared to the cumulative and combined wisdom expressed by all of the market participants as they buy or refrain from buying with money the state would otherwise take by taxation. C) Corruption, dishonesty and stupidity are rampant among people spending other peoples' money whereas those spending their own money are affected only by the latter. D) The utilization of land and assets acquired through taxation and owned by the state are going to be controlled by politics resulting in waste, divisiveness and discord among those contending in the political arena. E) All interference in the market by the state through taxation or regulation diverts resources away from their most productive utilization, thereby impoverishing—relatively speaking—all members of society, because only the market with its price structure can determine the highest–value utilization of scarce resources. F) A more knowledgeable (Austrian) economist could certainly provide a plethora of other reasons.

Rothschild's 25-Point Plan

1. Mankind is inclined to evil rather than good.

2. Preach Liberalism.

3. Use ideals of freedom to bring about class wars.

4. Any and all means necessary should be used to reach goals as they are justified.

5. Use force whenever necessary.

6. The power of resources must remain invisible until the very moment that strength is gained so no group or force can undermine it.

7. Advocate a mob psychology to obtain control of the masses.

8. Promote the use of alcohol, drugs, moral corruption, and all forms of vice to systematically corrupt the youth of the nation.

9. Seize citizens' private property by any means necessary.

10. Use slogans such as equity, liberty, and fraternity on the masses as psychological warfare.

11. War should be directed so that the nations on both sides are placed further in debt and peace conferences are designed so that neither combatant retain territory rights.

12. Members must use their wealth to have candidates chosen to public office who would be obedient to their demands, and would be used as pawns in the game by the men behind the scenes. The advisers will have been bred, reared, and trained from childhood to rule the affairs of the world.

13. Control the press, and hence most of the information the public receives.

14. Agents and provocateurs will come forward after creating traumatic situations, and appear to be the saviors of the masses, when they are actually interested in just the opposite, the reduction of the population.

15. Create industrial depression and financial panic, unemployment, hunger, and shortage of food. Use these events to control the masses and mobs. Use them to wipe out those who stand in the way.

16. Infiltrate Freemasonry which is to be used to conceal agendas and objectives.

17. Expound the value of systematic deception, use high sounding slogans and phrases, advocate lavish sounding promises to the masses even though they will not be kept.

18. The art of street fighting is necessary to bring the population into subjection.

19. Use agents as provocateurs and advisers behind the scenes, and after wars use secret diplomacy talks to gain control.

20. Establish huge monopolies toward world government control.

21. Use high taxes and unfair competition to bring about economic ruin by controlling raw materials, organized agitation among the workers, and subsidizing competitors.

22. Build up armaments with police and soldiers who can protect and further Illuminati interests.

23. Members and leaders of the one world government will be appointed by the director of the Illuminati.

24. Infiltrate into all classes and levels of society and government for the purpose of teaching the youth in the schools theories and principles known to be false.

25. Create and use national and international laws to destroy civilization.

Acknowledgments

I am forever grateful to God, the One Great Power. He is my greatest inspiration now and forevermore. He is the reason I wake up every morning and the same reason I am able to rest in peace and comfort. Without His spark of life I would be utterly nothing. He is my everything!

I would like to thank the following benevolent souls for their inspiration:

Jane Wolf, my lovely mother
Nicole Bielawski, a true best friend
Jon Fox, a friend to the end
Ned Netterville, a fellow tax protester
Raffi Thomas, a true brother of Spirit

Thank you to everyone who has crossed my path and into my life. I have the deepest gratitude for those who have contributed to my life's joys, struggles, and achievements.

And last, but not least, thank you dear reader for taking the time to read my book. It was a pleasure writing it. It was meant for you! I hope you enjoyed it.

About the Author

John Paul Mitchell is a graduate of the University of Sedona and holds a Ph.D. in Pastoral Counseling Psychology. He is a teacher of philosophy, meditation, and a firm advocate of non–state self–governance. He is the founder and master teacher of Illumina, a powerful self–mastery and meditation regimen.

John Paul has studied religious scripture and history since the age of twelve. He began meditating in high school and has been practicing for the last fifteen years. Since 1999 he has taught Yoga, meditation, and religious philosophy.

At the time of writing and publishing this book, he currently resides in Phoenix, Arizona.

More Information

If you are interested to learn more about the tax resistance movement and the state of our global economies, please visit the official *Tax Free World* website on the Internet.

www.taxfreeworld.org

Voice Your Opinion

The author of this book has conveniently setup a telephone number and voicemail system to leave your opinion about the content and message of the book. Feel free to call and leave a voicemail with your feelings and thoughts about taxation, the economy, monetary and banking systems, and your government. From time to time, we will select a voicemail to publish on the book's official website. Let your voice be heard:

(646) 961-3592

Index

Adams, John, 50

Adams, Samuel, 49

American Revolution, 47

Apostle Matthew, 26

Apostle Peter, 13, 23

Apostles, The, 26

apportionment, 65, 71

Artaxerxes I, 16, 19

Babylon, 52

Bank of England, 54–56

Bank of North America, 56

Bank of the United States, 56

bankers, 3, 15, 60

banking, 52, 56, 59

Bastiat, Frederic, 25

Battle of Concord, 49

Battle of Lexington, 49

Bauer, Mayer Amschel, 54

Bible, 6

Black Hand, 2

bondage, 37

Boston Tea Party, 49

British Parliament, 46, 48

Caesar, 10, 12, 44, 92

Caesar Augustus, 44

Capernaum, 13, 21, 23

capital punishment, 6

census, 66, 68

central bank, 3, 53, 57, 63

centurion, 21

Chodorov, Frank, 35

civil liberties, 85

civilization, 1

civilizations, 41

colonists, 48, 50, 55

compliance, 1, 11

Congress, 50, 57, 65

corruption, 71

crimes, 87

crucifixion, 6, 52

Currency Act, 48

democracy, 88

democratic republic, 88

dictatorship, 2

direct taxes, 67

disobedience, 11

donations, 43

economic depression, 61

economic recession, 61

economy, 59, 76, 87

Egibi, Jacob, 52

Egypt, 41, 52

enemy combatant, 3

England, 53

Europe, 54, 55

exports, 44

extortion, 2, 36

Ezra, 16, 19

fascism, 2

federal income tax, 50, 67

Federal Reserve, 2, 3, 60, 63

Federal Reserve Act, 57

federal taxes, 24

foreign bankers, 63

forgiveness, 87

Founding Fathers, 46, 50, 57

Fourth Amendment, 71

fractional reserve banking, 59

Frankfurt, 54

Franklin, Benjamin, 50

freedom, 85, 86

gain, 66, 67

Galilee, 6, 21, 22

Gandhi, Mahatma, 86

Germany, 54

God, 9, 25, 28, 32, 37

gold, 3

Golden Rule, 34

Gospels, 14

government, 1, 69, 75

governor, 5, 6

Grace Commission, 63

Great Britain, 45, 47, 49

Greece, 22, 42

half shekel, 15

Hamilton, Alexander, 55

Hancock, John, 50

heaven, 33

Henry, Patrick, 48

Herod, 6

Herodians, 10, 11

High Priest, 14

history, 41

homelessness, 87

Horus, 42

human rights, 34

humanitarian, 34

humanity, 86

Illumina, 33

Illuminati, 54

imports, 44

income, 66, 67, 83

income tax, 50

inflation, 58, 60

inscription, 12

interest rates, 59

Internal Revenue Code, 72

IRS, 2, 69, 72

Israel, 11, 15

Israelites, 19

Jackson, Andrew, 56

Jefferson, Thomas, 50, 51, 55

Jericho, 27

Jerusalem, 11, 14, 22

Jesus, 13, 23, 32

Jewish Court, 28

Jewish Temple, 11, 13, 14, 52

Jews, 5, 11, 13, 15

Judah, 11

Judea, 11, 21, 22, 28

Julius Caesar, 44

King Charles I, 45

King James I, 53

King William III, 53

kingdom, 28

kings, 53

Knox, Philander Chase, 65

Law, The, 25

leaders, 37

legislation, 1

liberty, 35, 37, 88

manipulation, 1

mankind, 37

messenger, 32

Messiah, 5, 6

military, 3

ministry, 10

money, 59, 81, 83

national debt, 51, 57, 64

Nero, 45

New Testament, 6, 14

North America, 47

Oliver Cromwell, 46

Otis, James, 48

Passover, 15
Patterson, William, 53, 55
Paul, Ron, 57
Pharaoh, 41
Pharisees, 10, 11, 26
Plumer, William, 51
Pompey, 11
Pontius Pilate, 6, 32
private banking, 52
Psalms, 29

Queen Boadicea, 44

Reagan, Ronald, 63, 64
rebellion, 12
Red Sea, 52
Renaissance, 53
resistance, 1
respectfulness, 34, 37
responsibility, 34, 37
resurrection, 52
Revenue Act, 65
revenues, 42, 66
revolution, 47
Revolutionary War, 46, 47, 49
riots, 46

Roman Empire, 11, 12, 44, 52
Roman poll tax, 5
Rome, 11, 44, 103
Rothschild, 54, 55, 108
Rothschild, Nathan Mayer, 55

Sanhedrin, 14, 23, 28
Saxons, 45
Schiff, Irwin, 79
scripture, 9
self-governance, 88
self-ownership, 33, 34
Senate, 3, 63
Senate Finance Committee, 69
Seven Years' War, 47
silver, 3
sinners, 25
Sixteenth Amendment, 57, 66
slavery, 68
slaves, 44
social programs, 68, 87
Sons of Liberty, 49
sovereign individual, 31
spiritual paths, 37
Stamp Act, 48
stealing, 29, 36, 37, 86
stock market, 61

Sugar Act, 48

Supreme Court, 50, 66, 67

synagogue, 21, 22

tax collectors, 25, 26

tax cuts, 87

tax evasion, 11, 24

tax protester, 6, 23, 24

tax resistance, 73, 79, 86

tax return, 78

tax revolt, 73, 85

taxation, 2, 73

taxpayers, 64, 72

theft, 36, 37

Torah, 14, 16, 21

torture, 6

treason, 3

trial, 52

U.S. Constitution, 57

U.S. Treasury, 64, 72, 73

usury, 53

wages, 65, 77, 87

war, 3, 47, 49, 68

wealth, 86

wealthy, 58

Weishaupt, Adam, 54

welfare, 36, 68, 87

Wilson, Woodrow, 65

Zacchaeus, 27, 28

www.ingramcontent.com/pod-product-compliance
Lightning Source LLC
Chambersburg PA
CBHW030022290326
41934CB00005B/448